IN SEARCH OF CHRISTMAS

God spoke His eternal wisdom to man in nature, whispered it through their souls, wrote it in His Word, and shouted it through His prophets. Then, in an act of grace and mercy, God sent His Only Begotten Son to earth. He left the glories of heaven to bring true love to humanity. Neither time nor space, nor even eternity, can contain such a love, for it flows like a river to water the souls of generation after generation. --- PAMELA KENNEDY

In Search of
Christmas

He is the Ancient Wisdom of the World,
The Word Creative, Beautiful and True,
The Nameless of Innumerable Names,
Ageless forever, yet Forever New.

CHARLES CARROLL ALBERTSON

IDEALS PUBLICATIONS
NASHVILLE, TENNESSEE

First printed in this format in 2005

ISBN 0-8249-5868-3

Published by Ideals Publications
A division of Guideposts
535 Metroplex Drive, Suite 250
Nashville, Tennessee 37211
www.idealsbooks.com

Color separations by Precision Color Graphics, Franklin, Wisconsin

Printed and bound in Italy

Library of Congress Cataloging-in-Publication Data on file.

Publisher, Patricia A. Pingry
Art Director, Eve DeGrie
Assistant Editor, Amy Johnson
Permissions, Patsy Jay

Front cover painting: WISE MEN APPROACHING BETHLEHEM, Joseph Maniscalco.
Copyright by Ideals Publications

1 3 5 7 9 10 8 6 4 2

ACKNOWLEDGMENTS:

CARMICHAEL, AMY. "Friends Angelical" from *Toward Jerusalem*. First published in 1936. First American edition 1977. Used by permission of Christian Literature Crusade. COATSWORTH, ELIZABETH. "A Landlord Remembers" from *Country Poems*. Reprinted with the permission of Simon & Schuster Books for Young Readers, an imprint of Simon & Schuster Children's Publishing Division. Copyright © 1942 by Elizabeth Coatsworth; copyright renewed © 1970 by Elizabeth Coatsworth Beston. CROWELL, GRACE NOLL. "Joseph" and "Home to Nazareth." Used by permission of the author's estate. GAITHER, WILLIAM J. "There's Something about That Name." Words by William J. and Gloria Gaither. Copyright © 1970 by William J. Gaither, Inc. ASCAP. Used by permission of Gaither Copyright Management. KENNEDY, PAMELA. "Christmas Angel," "Joseph's Story," "The Second Christmas," and "A Shepherd's Tale." Used by permission of the author. L'ENGLE, MADELEINE. "O Simplicitas" from *The Weather of the Heart*. Copyright © 1978, 2001 by Crosswicks, Ltd. Used by permission of WaterBrook Press. MOORE, VIRGINIA BLANCK. "Christmas Tree." Used by permission of the author. RORKE, MARGARET. "Ponderings." Used by permission of the author's estate. TREECE, HENRY. "Christ Child" from *Collected Poems of Henry Treece*. Copyright © 1946 by Henry Treece. Used by permission of John Johnson Limited, Author's Agent. UNTERMEYER, LOUIS. "The Donkey of God" from *Donkey of God*, Universe, 1999. Published by arrangement with the Estate of Louis Untermeyer, Norma Anchin Untermeyer, c/o Professional Publishing Services Company. Permission expressly granted by Laurence S. Untermeyer. Our sincere thanks to the following authors whom we were unable to locate: Alonzo Newton Benn for "Three Wise Men Journeyed"; Padraic Colum for "A Cradle Song"; John Duffy for "The Annunciation"; Calvin LeCompte for "The Visitation"; Jessie Wilmore Murton for "Bethlehem of Judea"; Frederick H. Sterne for "Magnificat" from *The Magic of the Manger*; Nancy Byrd Turner for "The Christmas Star"; B.Y. Williams for "Who Are the Wise Men?"

Contents

The search for Christmas begins, not on the day of the Nativity, but in the beginning of Genesis, through the prophetic voices of Scripture, beyond the good news of the Gospels, and culminates in the hope of the return of the Saviour to take His own to their eternal home.

The Master Plan

> *By a Carpenter mankind was made, and only by that Carpenter can mankind be remade.*
>
> Desiderius Erasmus

Chapter One

In the beginning was the Word, and the Word was with God, and the Word was God. The same was in the beginning with God. All things were made by him; and without him was not any thing made that was made. --- JOHN 1:1-3

A HYMN ON THE NATIVITY OF MY SAVIOUR

BEN JONSON

I sing the birth was born tonight,
The author both of life and light;
The angels so did sound it.
And like the ravished shepherds said,
Who saw the light and were afraid,
Yet searched, and true they found it.

The Son of God, the eternal king,
That did us all salvation bring,
And freed the soul from danger:
He whom the whole world could not take,
The Word, which heaven and earth did make,
Was now laid in a manger.

The Father's wisdom willed it so,
The Son's obedience knew no No,
Both wills were in one stature;
And as that wisdom had decreed,
The Word was now made flesh indeed,
And took on Him our Nature.

What comfort by Him do we win,
Who made Himself the price of sin,
To make us heirs of glory!
To see this babe all innocence,
A martyr born in our defence—
Can man forget the story?

THE NATIVITY by Julius Gari Melchers. Peter Harholdt/Superstock.

THE ADORATION OF THE SHEPHERDS: attributed to Denys Calvaert. Christie's Images.

In the beginning God created the heaven and the earth. And the earth was without form, and void; and darkness was upon the face of the deep. And the Spirit of God moved upon the face of the waters. And God said, Let there be light: and there was light. And God saw the light, that it was good: and God divided the light from the darkness. And God called the light Day, and the darkness he called Night. And the evening and the morning were the first day. --- GENESIS 1:1-5

ON THE MORNING OF CHRIST'S NATIVITY

JOHN MILTON

This is the month, and this the happy morn,
Wherein the Son of Heaven's eternal King,
Of wedded maid and virgin mother born,
Our great redemption from above did bring;
For so the holy sages once did sing,
    That he our deadly forfeit should release,
And with his Father work us a perpetual peace.

That glorious form, that light unsufferable,
And that far-beaming blaze of majesty,
Wherewith he wont at Heaven's high council-table
To sit the midst of Trinal Unity,
He laid aside; and here with us to be,
    Forsook the courts of everlasting day,
And chose with us a darksome house of mortal clay.

And God said, Let the earth bring forth grass, and the herb yielding seed, and the fruit tree yielding fruit after his kind, whose seed is in itself, upon the earth: and it was so. And the earth brought forth grass, and herb yielding seed after his kind, and the tree yielding fruit. --- GENESIS 1:11-12

CHRISTMAS TREE

VIRGINIA BLANCK MOORE

A tree, the verdant evergreen,
Is mute testimony that some things on earth
Do not change as the seasons,
And the centuries come and go;
That in this world of change
Something abiding, enduring, unvariable
Has been provided.

For this reason it is fitting
That the evergreen be used as the symbol of Christmas,
The season when we celebrate the birth
Of the One whose love is
Unchanging, unflagging, and steadfast;
A love which, like the evergreen,
Whatever the season,
Remains ever verdant.

So each evergreen tree,
Gay in its holiday dress,
Proclaims to us the unfailing nature
Of the love of Him who was born
In the manger at Bethlehem.

MADONNA PRAYING by Francesco Botticini. Superstock.

THE ADORATION OF THE SHEPHERDS: attributed to Willem Van Herp. Christie's Images.

And God said, Let there be lights in the firmament of the heaven. . . . And God made two great lights; the greater light to rule the day. . . . he made the stars also. --- GENESIS 1:14, 16

A CHRISTMAS CAROL

G.K. CHESTERTON

The Christ Child lay on Mary's lap,
His hair was like a light.
(O weary, weary was the world,
But here is all aright.)

The Christ Child lay on Mary's breast,
His hair was like a star.
(O stern and cunning are the kings,
But here the true hearts are.)

The Christ Child lay on Mary's heart,
His hair was like a fire.
(O weary, weary is the world,
But here the world's desire.)

The Christ Child stood at Mary's knee,
His hair was like a crown,
And all the flowers looked up at Him,
And all the stars looked down.

And God created great whales, and every living creature that moveth. . . . And God said, Let the earth bring forth the living creature after his kind, cattle, and creeping thing, and beast of the earth after his kind. --- GENESIS 1:21, 24

THE FRIENDLY BEASTS

OLD ENGLISH CAROL

Jesus our brother, kind and good,
Was humbly born in a stable rude,
And friendly beasts around him stood.
Jesus our brother, kind and good.

"I," said the donkey, shaggy and brown,
"I carried his mother uphill and down;
I carried her safely to Bethlehem town."
"I," said the donkey, shaggy and brown.

"I," said the cow, all white and red,
"I gave him my manger for a bed;
I gave him my hay to pillow his head."
"I," said the cow, all white and red.

"I," said the sheep with curly horn,
"I gave him my wool for his blanket warm;

He wore my coat on Christmas morn."
"I," said the sheep with curly horn.

"I," said the dove from the rafters high,
"Cooed him to sleep that he should not cry;
We cooed him to sleep, my mate and I."
"I," said the dove from the rafters high.

"I," said the camel, yellow and black,
"Over the desert upon my back,
I brought him a gift in the wise men's pack."
"I," said the camel, yellow and black.

Thus every beast by some good spell
In the stable dark was glad to tell
Of the gift he gave Emmanuel,
The gift he gave Emmanuel.

CHRISTMAS by Fra Diamante. Erich Lessing/Art Resource.

THE DONKEY OF GOD

LOUIS UNTERMEYER

At the time of this story, Italy was not one country as she is today. Italy was divided into many provinces, each of them jealous of the other. There was not even a united feeling within the provinces themselves. In the Middle Ages every city had its own government, and every city hated its neighbors. Assisi claimed to be the oldest of the hill-towns. It boasted of tombs that were even older than the temple-ruins; its vine-terraced slopes grew the richest grapes and the juiciest olives. Assisi was a happy place. It was even a merry one. Its merchants were wealthy, its churches were richly decorated, its young people were dressed as though life were one long carnival.

Of all the gay youths, none was as richly costumed as Francis. His father was a cloth-merchant and Francis was his favorite son. No wonder his horse was the swiftest, his cap-feather the longest, his armor the handsomest, and his eyes the most impudent in Assisi. When, after an uncomfortable peace, the neighboring cities threatened a new war, no one was quicker to call for action than the bold son of the cloth-merchant.

"Let us not wait until Perugia comes out against us," cried Francis. "Let us carry the war into her own fields, against her own gates. Let our swords break down her pride; let torches lay waste the old enemy. On to Perugia!"

A little past midnight, the army from Assisi set out to surprise the foe. But the Perugians must have had the same idea, for that night the Umbrian plain held two armies marching against each other. It was still dark when they met. The surprise was complete and all plans of orderly battle vanished with the first blow. They fought recklessly in a blackness lit only by torches. With the first streak of dawn, the fight came to an end. The scene was horrible beyond description. Each army had killed more of its own men than the enemy's. The stoutest of horsemen felt sick.

None felt sicker than Francis. He had seen things that turned his ideas upside down. His heart felt as though an unseen dagger had run through it. With the dawn something new had dawned in Francis, something that would not die. For weeks he lay tossing in a high fever. The doctors could do nothing to make him rest. Francis would start from a short sleep, call out, and lie awake the rest of the night, crying things that no one could understand. He was wasting away; his condition seemed hopeless. On the fortieth day, after the doctors had shaken their heads and gone, Francis got up. No one saw him go. He walked out of the house at dawn as softly as the light that showed him the way. Assisi was just awaking as he passed through the crooked streets and out of town.

It was a different Francis that wandered, silently and alone, past the Umbrian plain. The rich suit had been exchanged for a coarse brown frock; instead of a sword he carried a wooden staff; there were no ornaments on his sleeves, no feathers on his hat—even the hat was gone. The impudent look had vanished from his eyes, the lines of boastfulness had left his lips.

Following some inner guide, he took passage on a boat and landed on the island of Sardinia. Here, far from the frivolous life of his past, he learned to live. One day, as he was walking, he noticed a donkey standing in the shade of a stunted tree, but it did not appear in the least astonished to see him. Now that he observed it closer, he could not remember ever having seen a donkey so small. It was no larger than a large dog, a sheep-dog with unusually long ears. Its ankles were more delicate than a deer's and the eyes had a speaking softness. But the most peculiar feature was a pattern made by two intersecting lines of black, one line running down the back from head to tail, the other line running across the shoulders. Presently, Francis noticed that the animal was speaking to him and he was aware that he understood it.

"Tell me, my good man," it was saying, "for I can see you are good, is there no justice in creation? Isn't it bad enough that we donkeys have to carry every sort of burden—twice as much as the horse—without also being a joke among men and animals? Is that just? And if that were not enough, why should we be made still more foolish by having to wear such a disfiguring pattern on our back? Can you answer that?"

To his surprise, Francis heard himself replying to the little donkey as if he were a priest and it were one of his flock. "Yes, my daughter, I think I can. There is a justice in all things, though we cannot see it at once. We must wait until the pattern is completed before we judge any of its parts. In your case the answer is easier than most, for you are the donkey of God." And Francis, who had never seen the creature before, and who certainly had never thought of its origin, heard himself telling this strange legend:

It was the morning of the Sixth Day. God had spent the First Day inventing Light. On the Second Day God had designed the seas. On the

Third Day, being dissatisfied with the emptiness of a world of water, He had gathered the waters in one place and had put dry land carefully among the seas. On the Fourth Day God had looked at the widespread Heaven and realized it needed something. So He had put lights in it: a great gold light to rule the day, and a soft silver one to rule the night. On the Fifth Day He decided He wanted more motion and sound in the universe. So He had filled the waters with whales and minnows and the air with insects and eagles.

Now it was the Sixth Day. The earth, God saw, needed life no less than sea and sky. So early in the morning He began making animals. First He made small simple ones: the snake and the snail, the mouse and the mole, rat and rabbit, cat and dog, and a hundred others, each after his kind. He tried the same design on an ever-growing scale. It was then He made donkey and deer, horse and cattle, lion and tiger, bear, buffalo, and elk. In the afternoon He looked at everything and said, "It is good." After a little while He added, "But it could be better. It lacks something. I will take the very best soil from the earth, I will mix it with water, I will knead it with air. I will then put a spark of Myself deep in him so he may be God-like. And it will be Man."

When the animals heard this, they began arguing with God. While the others were arguing or grumbling among themselves, the donkey calmly went on eating and growing lovelier every minute. Perhaps I should have told you that he had been born the most perfect of four-footed creatures. He was very much like the donkeys of today except that his color was softer, his eyes more tender, his ankles even more graceful—and at that time, the long ears of his great-great-grandchildren did not disguise his head.

The donkey was so busy eating that he did not see God make the first man. The next morning—it was Sunday—the other animals told him about it and said the man-animal was called Adam and the woman-animal was called Eve. A little tired of doing nothing but eating, the donkey joined the other beasts and peered into the garden where the two newest-born creatures were sitting. When he saw them he burst into the loudest and most ridiculous laugh on earth.

"Ho-hee-haw!" screamed the donkey. "It was *too* funny! *Such* animals! They're made all wrong! No hide! No hoofs! Not even a tail! And so pink—so *naked!* God must have meant to put a coat of fleece on them and forgot it! Ho-hee-*haw!*"

This was too much for Adam. He ran over to the donkey and grasped him by the ears. The donkey tried to pull himself free, but Adam held fast. As he tugged and Adam tightened, his ears began to stretch, grow longer. . . . And while they were pulling, God suddenly appeared. Said the Lord, "Because you have spoiled My day of rest and because you have made fun of My creation you shall be punished. You shall serve man and be subject to him all the days of your life."

So it was decreed. And so it turned out. When Adam and Eve were forced to leave the Garden and go to work, the donkey went with them. Adam rode on the horse, the dog trotted at Eve's side, but it was the donkey who carried the tools, the spinning-wheel, and all the household machinery. The donkey wondered how long the burdens would be piled upon him.

After Adam died, the donkey thought things would go easier, but he soon realized his hardships were only beginning. He belonged, he discovered, not to one man but to all men. Cain, the brutal son of Adam, broke him to harness and made him drag the heavy plow. When Noah built the ark the donkey carried more timber than the elephant, but no one praised him for it. He crossed the Red Sea with Moses; he was beaten for trying to save the wizard Balaam; he entered Canaan with Joshua.

He worked; he wandered; he did not die.

Years passed; centuries vanished. The donkey was in Palestine. His master was a carpenter in the little town of Nazareth, a good master by the name of Joseph. He had worked for him a long time, and he had served his owner well. A few years ago, when Joseph and his wife Mary were on their wanderings, the little donkey carried them everywhere without complaining. They were terribly poor and the innkeepers had no room for them. The donkey trudged on, carrying his load that seemed to grow heavier with each step. For a long day and longer night he plodded toward the distant haven, never stopping or stumbling till he brought them to the little town of Bethlehem. That night, in a cattle-stall, Mary's child had been born.

More years passed. Jesus had gone away. Though the donkey did not know it, the carpenter's son had grown from childhood to manhood, had traveled and studied, had healed the sick, restored eyesight to the blind, suffered untold hardships. But now the moment had come; Jesus was to enter Jerusalem in triumph.

It was a tremendous moment; one that must be celebrated in the proper manner. Naturally, Jesus could not enter the city of Palestine on foot; he must ride, they said, on a charger worthy of the event. So the Archangel Michael called all the animals before Jesus that they might plead their case.

"Choose me," said the lion. "I am the king of beasts; you are a king among men. Men respect royalty—but only when they recognize it! When the people of Jerusalem see you riding on my back, they will know you are of noble blood and they will bow down and fear you."

"Choose me," said the eagle. "I am lord of the upper air. When you enter Jerusalem flying between my strong wings, the people will believe you are a god and they will worship."

"Choose me! Choose me!" cried the animals separately and in chorus. Only the donkey was silent.

"And what can you give?" asked Jesus, speaking for the first time and turning to the dusty little fellow. "What have you to promise?"

"Nothing," murmured the donkey. "Nothing. I am the lowest of all God's creatures and the least."

But Jesus remembered. "The lowest shall be lifted up," he said. "And the last shall be first."

And so the meekest of men chose the meekest of animals. And they entered Jerusalem together. But the great moment passed. Proud Jerusalem sneered at the carpenter's son even as it had stoned the prophets before him, and only a handful of poor folk listened to his words. He was despised and rejected. The people turned against him. He was imprisoned on a false charge and condemned to death. They put a crown of thorns upon his head, mocked him, and made him carry his own cross.

It was while Jesus was struggling up the hill that the donkey saw him for the last time. Their sad eyes met.

"No," said Jesus. "You cannot help me now. Yet, since you have done more for me than have most men, you shall be rewarded. I cannot undo what God has done; what He has ordained must be carried out. But I can soften His decree. True, you will have to fetch and carry and feed on thorns. Yet these things will never again be hard for you. You bore me when I grew to manhood, when I was a child, and even my mother before I was born. So shall you bear my cross, but you shall bear it without pain. Here—!" And as Jesus touched the shoulders of the donkey, a velvet-black cross appeared on the back of the kneeling animal. And Jesus, shouldering his burden, climbed up Calvary. . . .

Francis heard the last syllable leave his lips in a kind of wonder. His tiredness had gone: everything in him was full of strength. He was surprised to see that the sun had set and that a little horned moon had come into the sky, one horn pointing to Assisi. He thought he understood the sign. When he turned back, the donkey had disappeared. The field was dark. But a light greater than the moon's was on Francis' face.

And God said, Let us make man in our image. . . . And the LORD God planted a garden eastward in Eden; and there he put the man whom he had formed. . . . And the LORD God commanded the man, saying, Of every tree of the garden thou mayest freely eat: But of the tree of the knowledge of good and evil, thou shalt not eat of it: for in the day that thou eatest thereof thou shalt surely die. . . . And the LORD God said, Behold, the man is become as one of us, to know good and evil: and now, lest he put forth his hand, and take also of the tree of life, and eat, and live for ever: Therefore the LORD God sent him forth from the garden of Eden . . . and he placed at the east of the garden of Eden Cherubims, and a flaming sword which turned every way, to keep the way of the tree of life.

--- GENESIS 1:26, 2:8, 16-17, 3:22-24

MOONLESS DARKNESS

GERARD MANLEY HOPKINS

Moonless darkness stands between.
Past, O Past, no more be seen!
But the Bethlehem star may lead me
To the sight of Him who freed me
From the self that I have been.

Make me pure, Lord: Thou art holy;
Make me meek, Lord: Thou wert lowly;
Now beginning, and alway:
Now begin,
On Christmas Day.

ADORATION OF THE MAGI by Christian W.E. Dietrich. Gemaldegalerie/Superstock.

DEPICTION OF JESUS IN THE TEMPLE by Giovanni Bellini. Pinacoteca Querini-Stampalia/Superstock.

And the Word was made flesh, and dwelt among us, And we beheld his glory, the glory as of the only begotten of the Father. --- JOHN 1:14

LOVE DIVINE, ALL LOVES EXCELLING

CHARLES WESLEY

Love Divine, all loves excelling,
Joy of heav'n, to earth come down;
Fix in us thy humble dwelling;
All thy faithful mercies crown.

Jesus, thou art all compassion,
Pure, unbounded love thou art;
Visit us with thy salvation;
Enter ev'ry trembling heart.

Joy to the World

Isaac Watts

George Frederick Handel

Joy to the world! the Lord is come; Let earth re-

ceive her King; Let ev' - ry heart pre - pare him

room, And heav'n and na - ture sing; And heav'n and na - ture

sing, And heav'n and heav'n and na - ture sing.

THE REST ON THE FLIGHT INTO EGYPT by Sebastiano Ricci. Christie's Images.

Joy to the earth! The Saviour reigns;
Let men their songs employ,
While fields and floods,
Rocks, hills, and plains
Repeat the sounding joy;
Repeat the sounding joy,
Repeat, repeat, the sounding joy.

No more let sin
And sorrow grow,
Nor thorns infest the ground;
He comes to make his blessings flow
Far as the curse is found;
Far as the curse is found,
Far as, far as the curse is found.

He rules the world
With truth and grace
And makes the nations prove
The glories of his righteousness
And wonders of his love;
And wonders of his love,
And wonders, wonders of his love.

The Prophecy

Christmas began in the heart of God.
It is complete only when it reaches
the heart of man.
VANCE HAVNER

CHAPTER TWO

Comfort ye, comfort ye my people, saith your God. . . . Prepare ye the way of the LORD, make straight in the desert a highway for our God. Every valley shall be exalted, and every mountain and hill shall be made low: and the crooked shall be made straight, and the rough places plain: And the glory of the LORD shall be revealed, and all flesh shall see it together: for the mouth of the LORD hath spoken it. --- ISAIAH 40:1, 3-5

COME, O LONG EXPECTED JESUS

CHARLES WESLEY

Come, O long expected Jesus,
Born to set your people free;
From our fears and sins release us;
Free us from captivity.

Israel's strength and consolation,
You, the hope of all the earth,
Dear desire of ev'ry nation,
Come and save us by your birth.

Born your people to deliver;
Born a child and yet a king!
Born to reign in us forever,
Now your gracious kingdom bring.

By your own eternal Spirit
Rule in all our hearts alone;
By your all sufficient merit
Raise us to your glorious throne.

ADORATION OF THE SHEPHERDS: DETAIL by Jacob Jordaens. Superstock.

For, behold, the darkness shall cover the earth, and gross darkness the people: but the LORD shall arise upon thee, and his glory shall be seen upon thee. . . . The people that walked in darkness have seen a great light: they that dwell in the land of the shadow of death, upon them hath the light shined. --- ISAIAH 60:2, 9:2

THY KINGDOM COME

BERNARD OF CLAIRVAUX

Thou hope of all the lowly!
To thirsting souls how kind!
Gracious to all who seek Thee,
Oh, what to those who find!

My tongue but lisps Thy praises,
Yet praise be my employ;
Love makes me bold to praise Thee,
For Thou art all my joy.

In Thee my soul delighting,
Findeth her only rest;
And so in Thee confiding,
May all the world be blest!

Dwell with us, and our darkness
Will flee before Thy light;
Scatter the world's deep midnight,
And fill it with delight.

O all mankind! behold Him
And seek His love to know;
And let your hearts, in seeking,
Be fired with love and glow!

O come, O come, great Monarch,
Eternal glory Thine;
The longing world waits for Thee!
Arise, arise and shine!

ANNUNCIATION TO THE SHEPHERDS by Jacopo Bassano. Belvoir Castle/Superstock.

THE HOLY FAMILY by Bartolomé Esteban Murillo. Scala/Art Resource.

And there shall come forth a rod out of the stem of Jesse, and a Branch shall grow out of his roots: And the spirit of the LORD shall rest upon him, the spirit of wisdom and understanding, the spirit of counsel and might, the spirit of knowledge and of the fear of the LORD. --- ISAIAH 11:1, 2

COME, LORD, AND TARRY NOT

HORATIUS BONAR

Come, Lord, and tarry not!
Bring the long looked-for day!
O why these years of waiting here,
These ages of delay?

Come, for your saints still wait;
Daily ascends their sigh;
The Spirit and the Bride say,
"Come!" Do you not hear the cry?

Come, for creation groans,
Impatient of your stay,

Worn out with these long years of ill,
These ages of delay.

Come, and make all things new,
Build up this ruined earth;
Restore our faded paradise,
Creation's second birth.

Come, and begin your reign
Of everlasting peace;
Come, take the kingdom to yourself,
Great King of righteousness!

Therefore the LORD himself shall give you a sign;
Behold, a virgin shall conceive, and bear a son, and shall
call his name Immanuel. --- ISAIAH 7:14

THE ANNUNCIATION

JOHN DUFFY

And was it true, the stranger standing so,
And saying things that lifted her in two?
Her eyes filled slowly with the morning glow.
Her drowsy ear drank in a first sweet dubious bird.

Although the morning beams
Came spilling in the gradual
    rubric known to every day,
And hills stood black and ruinous as in eclipse
Against the softly spreading ray,
Not touched by any strange apocalypse
Though nothing was disturbed
    from where she lay and saw,
Now she remembered with a quick
    and panting awe
That someone came, and took in hand her heart,
And broke it irresistibly apart
With what he said, and how in tall suspense

He lingered while the white celestial inference,
Pushing her fears apart, went softly home.

Never again would she awake
And find herself the buoyant Galilean lass,
But into her dissolving dreams would break
A hovering consciousness too terrible to pass:
A new awareness in her body when she stirred,
A sense of Light within her virgin gloom.
She was the mother of the wandering Word,
Little and terrifying in her laboring womb.

And nothing would again be casual and small,
But everything with light invested, overspilled
With terror and divinity, the dawn,
    the first bird's call,
The silhouetted pitcher waiting to be filled.

THE ANNUNCIATION by William Bouguereau. Christie's Images.

For unto us a child is born, unto us a son is given: and the government shall be upon his shoulder: and his name shall be called Wonderful, Counsellor, The mighty God, The everlasting Father, The Prince of Peace. --- ISAIAH 9:6

IT IS COMING TONIGHT

PHILLIPS BROOKS

The earth has grown old with its burden of care,
But at Christmas it always is young.
The heart of the jewel burns lustrous and fair,
And its soul full of music bursts forth on the air,
When the song of the angels is sung.

It is coming, Old Earth, it is coming tonight!
On the snowflakes that cover thy sod.
The feet of the Christ Child fall gentle and white,
And the voice of the Christ Child tells out with delight
That mankind are the children of God.

On the sad and the lonely, the wretched and poor,
That voice of the Christ Child shall fall;
And to every blind wanderer opens the door
Of hope which he dared not to dream of before,
With a sunshine and welcome for all.

The feet of the humblest may walk in the field
Where the feet of the Holiest have trod;
This, then, is the marvel to mortals revealed,
When the silvery trumpets of Christmas have pealed,
That mankind are the children of God.

HOLY NIGHT by Antonio Allegri Correggio. Erich Lessing/Art Resource.

A SHEPHERD'S TALE

PAMELA KENNEDY

A ndrew walked slowly up the hillside behind the city of Bethlehem. His right hand clutched a shepherd's staff, and his left hand held the gnarled fingers of his blind grandfather, Benjamin. Benjamin had tended the flocks for over forty years; and now that he could no longer see, Andrew, the youngest of his grandsons, was assigned to accompany him to the hills. Day after day and night after night, Andrew was his grandfather's eyes, counting and describing the sheep, guiding the old, calloused hands over the animals so the seasoned shepherd could assess the condition of his flock.

Sometimes, though, his grandfather would tell him stories from the Scriptures. This afternoon, as the sheep grazed and the sun neared the horizon, Benjamin was droning on about Isaiah; how the prophet had said that a great king was coming to rule God's people with justice and truth. Andrew drifted into a dreamless sleep.

Benjamin's cry awoke Andrew with a start, and the boy scrambled to his feet, disoriented from sleep and shielding his eyes from the dazzling light that burned in the sky.

"What is it?" the old man whispered in fear.

"I'm not sure," Andrew replied. "It's like the sky is on fire; but there's no heat, just brightness. Oh, Grandfather!"

"What's happening? Tell me, Andrew!"

"I don't know, Grandfather. It looks like people, men in robes, flying in the light."

At that moment, the night was shattered by joyous singing. It was as if the sky had broken in two and music poured out from the heart of the heavens. Chords and harmonies unfamiliar to earthly ears swept around the hillside and lifted the leaves and grasses in a burst of melody. Then words became distinguishable: "Fear not, for . . . unto you is born this day in the city of David a Saviour, which is Christ the Lord. . . . Ye shall find the babe wrapped in swaddling clothes, lying in a manger."

Then a chorus began to roll over the hillside like a wave: "Glory to God in the highest, and on earth peace, good will toward men."

"It has happened," Benjamin whispered. "He has come. The Messiah has come at last. Oh, praise God!" And Benjamin fell to his knees on the grassy ground.

The other shepherds began to murmur among themselves. Finally, one of them spoke with conviction. "I think we should go and see this thing."

"But how do we know where to go?" asked another.

"The angel said the child would be in a manger," Benjamin said, "wrapped in cloth and lying in a manger in Bethlehem. It is just as the prophets have written! Come, Andrew, give me your hand."

The two started down the hillside and traveled through the darkened streets of Bethlehem, Benjamin navigating as if led by some inner compass. Before long, they came to a small inn which appeared to be locked and shuttered for the night. Benjamin whispered to his grandson, "Come, it is here."

Skirting the building, they approached the rocky, cavelike stable at the back. They came upon a startled couple, kneeling in the straw.

Falling to his knees again, Benjamin spoke to the couple he could not see. "We have come to worship the Messiah. Is it as Isaiah said: 'Behold, a virgin shall conceive, and bear a son, and shall call him Immanuel'?"

Andrew watched the young mother as her eyes warmed with understanding at the old man's words. Gently, she lowered the infant into Benjamin's arms, and Andrew saw his grandfather's body tremble at the touch of the tiny babe.

"It is he," the mother whispered, and tears slipped from the sightless eyes as Benjamin held the hope of Israel against his breast.

Later, Andrew could not recall how long they had lingered in the stable. Time seemed to have little meaning that night. No one spoke as they settled back onto the familiar rocks and wrapped their robes about them.

When the rosy pink of dawn slipped up the morning sky, Benjamin broke the stillness. "Andrew," he said, "bring me that newborn lamb." Extending one hand, he added, "the one to the right of the olive tree."

Hark! The Herald Angels Sing

Charles Wesley

Felix Mendelssohn

Hark! the her - ald an - gels sing, "Glo - ry to the new - born king.

Peace on earth and mer - cy mild, God and sin - ners re - con - ciled!"

Joy - ful, all ye na - tions, rise, Join the tri - umph of the skies;

With th'an - gel - ic host pro - claim, "Christ is born in Beth - le - hem!"

Hark! the her - ald an - gels sing, "Glo - ry to the new - born King."

Christ, by highest heaven adored.
Christ, the everlasting Lord!
Late in time behold him come,
Offspring of a virgin's womb.
Veiled in flesh the Godhead see;
Hail the incarnate Deity.
Pleased as man with men to dwell,
Jesus, our Immanuel!
Hark! the herald angels sing,
"Glory to the newborn King!"

Hail, the heaven-born Prince of Peace!
Hail, the Sun of Righteousness!
Light and life to all he brings,
Risen with healing in his wings.
Mild, he lays his glory by,
Born that man no more may die,
Born to raise the sons of earth,
Born to give them second birth.
Hark! the herald angels sing,
"Glory to the newborn King."

Come, Desire of nations, come,
Fix in us thy humble home;
Oh, to all thyself impart,
Formed in each believing heart!
Hark! the herald angels sing,
"Glory to the newborn King;
Peace on earth and mercy mild,
God and sinners reconciled!"
Hark! the herald angels sing,
"Glory to the newborn King!"

The Angels Proclaim

Christmas is the day that holds all time together.

ALEXANDER SMITH

CHAPTER THREE

Donne par M. Iean Durant preltost
De Mitry luiuan le contrat Du
XX. feurier 1652

And there appeared unto him an angel of the Lord . . . And when Zacharias saw him, he was troubled, and fear fell upon him. But the angel said unto him, Fear not, Zacharias: for thy prayer is heard; and thy wife Elisabeth shall bear thee a son, and thou shalt call his name John. . . . And he shall go before Him in the spirit . . . to make ready a people prepared for the Lord. . . . I am Gabriel, that stand in the presence of God. --- LUKE 1:11-13, 17, 19

FRIENDS ANGELICAL

AMY CARMICHAEL

Far beyond the shifting screen
Made of things that can be seen,
Are our friends angelical
Of the Land Celestial. . . .

What their toils we may not know,
As they come and as they go.
Only this we know: they see
As we cannot, what shall be. . . .
Therefore look behind the screen,
Trust the powers of the Unseen.
Neither vague nor mystical
Are our friends angelical.

APPARIZIONE DELL'ANGELO A ZACCARIA by Ghirlandaio Domenico. Art Resource.

And in the sixth month the angel Gabriel was sent from God unto a city of Galilee, named Nazareth, to a virgin espoused to a man whose name was Joseph, of the house of David; and the virgin's name was Mary. And the angel came in unto her, and said, Hail, thou that art highly favoured, the Lord is with thee: blessed art thou among women. And when she saw him, she was troubled at his saying, and cast in her mind what manner of salutation this should be. --- LUKE 1:26-29

THERE IS NO ROSE

AUTHOR UNKNOWN

There is no rose of such virtue
As is the rose that bare Jesus;
Alleluia.

For in this rose contained was
Heaven and earth in little space;
Res miranda.

By that rose we may well see
That He is God in persons three,
Pari forma.

The angels sang, the shepherds too:
Gloria in excelsis deo:
Gaudeamus.

Leave we all this worldly mirth,
And follow we this joyful birth;
Transeamus.

THE ANNUNCIATION by Guilio Cesare Procaccini. Bridgeman Art Library/Superstock.

THE ANNUNCIATION by Giovanni Odazzi. Christie's Images/Superstock.

And the angel said unto her, Fear not, Mary: for thou hast found favour with God. And, behold, thou shalt conceive in thy womb, and bring forth a son, and shalt call his name JESUS. He shall be great . . . and of his kingdom there shall be no end. --- LUKE 1:30-33

CHRISTMAS EVE CHORAL

BLISS CARMAN

Hallelujah!
What sound is this across the dark
While all the earth is sleeping? Hark!
Hallelujah! Hallelujah! Hallelujah!

Why are thy tender eyes so bright,
Mary, Mary?
"On the prophetic deep of night,
Joseph, Joseph,
I see the borders of the light,
And in the day that is to be
An aureoled man-child I see,
Great love's son, Joseph.
Hallelujah!"
He hears not, but she hears afar
The minstrel angel of the star.
Hallelujah! Hallelujah! Hallelujah!

Why is thy gentle smile so deep,
Mary, Mary?
"It is the secret I must keep,
Joseph, Joseph,

The joy that will not let me sleep,
The glory of the coming days,
When all the world shall turn to praise
God's goodness, Joseph.
Hallelujah!"
Clear as the bird that brings the morn
She hears the heavenly music borne.
Hallelujah! Hallelujah! Hallelujah!

Why is thy voice so strange and far,
Mary, Mary?
"I see the glory of the star,
Joseph, Joseph,
And in its light all things that are
Made glad and wise beyond the sway
Of death and darkness and dismay,
In God's time, Joseph.
Hallelujah!"
To every heart in love 'tis given
To hear the ecstasy of heaven.
Hallelujah! Hallelujah! Hallelujah!

Then said Mary unto the angel, How shall this be, seeing I know not a man? And the angel answered and said unto her, The Holy Ghost shall come upon thee, and the power of the Highest shall overshadow thee: therefore also that holy thing which shall be born of thee shall be called the Son of God. . . . And Mary said, Behold the handmaid of the Lord; be it unto me according to thy word. And the angel departed from her. --- Luke 1:34-35, 38

O Simplicitas

Madeleine L'Engle

An angel
Came to me
And I was unprepared
To be what God was using.
A moment I despaired,
Thought briefly of refusing.
The angel knew I heard.
According to God's Word
I bowed to this strange choosing.

A palace should have been
The birthplace of a king
(I had no way of knowing).
We went to Bethlehem;
It was so strange a thing.
The wind was cold, and blowing,
My cloak was old, and thin.
They turned us from the inn;
The town was overflowing.

God's Word, a child so small,
Who still must learn to speak,
Lay in humiliation.
Joseph stood, strong and tall.
The beasts were warm and meek
And moved with hesitation.
The Child born in a stall?
I understood it: all.
Kings came in adoration.

Perhaps it was absurd:
The stable set apart,
The sleepy cattle lowing;
And the incarnate Word
Resting against my heart.
My joy was overflowing.
The shepherds came, adored
The folly of the Lord,
Wiser than all men's knowing.

MADONNA IN PRAYER by Giovanni B.S. Sassoferrato. Superstock.

VISIT BETWEEN MARY AND ELIZABETH by David Passavant. Superstock.

And Mary arose in those days, and went into the hill country with haste, into a city of Juda; And entered into the house of Zacharias, and saluted Elisabeth. And it came to pass, that, when Elisabeth heard the salutation of Mary, the babe leaped in her womb; and Elisabeth was filled with the Holy Ghost: And she spake out with a loud voice, and said, Blessed art thou among women, and blessed is the fruit of thy womb. And whence is this to me, that the mother of my Lord should come to me? For, lo, as soon as the voice of thy salutation sounded in mine ears, the babe leaped in my womb for joy. --- LUKE 1:39-44

THE VISITATION

CALVIN LE COMPTE

To Elisabeth she came,
over the hills,
bearing the Lord
flowering in her womb—
sacrament of her flesh,
bud richly taut—
the warmth of her
containing His infinity,
the sun His fire.

The dark earth of her body
seemed to encompass all things.
The terraced fields of Judah
pregnant with seed

called out to her
as she passed,
praising the Child
she was yet to bear,
invoking His blessing
on their expectancy.

These must call out,
full in their fullness,
barren beside hers,
then how should a child
six months conceived
adore with stillness
in his mother's womb?

And Mary said, My soul doth magnify the Lord, And my spirit hath rejoiced in God my Saviour. For he hath regarded the low estate of his handmaiden: for, behold, from henceforth all generations shall call me blessed. For he that is mighty hath done to me great things; and holy is his name. --- LUKE 1:46-49

MAGNIFICAT

FREDERICK H. STERNE

And he shall suckle at my breast,
And lie upon my knee;
And he shall say his childhood prayer
And cuddle close to me;
And I shall tell him bible tales
Seated upon the sod;
Ah, wonder; that my baby boy
Should be the Son of God!

Of me, the maid of low estate,
Messiah must be born,
And yet men gaze with ribald mirth
And evil eyes of scorn.

The kindly neighbors draw apart
To whisper words of blame,
And patient Joseph, sad at heart,
Must share with me my shame.

Yet he shall sit on David's throne,
Inviolate of old;
And he shall be the promised seed
Of whom the prophet told.
My soul doth magnify the Lord,
My heart doth sing for joy;
Oh, wonder, that the Son of God
Should be my baby boy.

VIRGIN OF THE ANNUNCIATION by Bartolomé Esteban Murillo. Superstock.

THE VISION OF ZACHARIAS by James J. Tissot. Superstock.

Now Elisabeth's full time came that she should be delivered; and she brought forth a son. . . . And his mother answered and said . . . he shall be called John. . . . And his father Zacharias was filled with the Holy Ghost, and prophesied, saying, Blessed be the Lord God of Israel; for he hath visited and redeemed his people. --- LUKE 1:57, 60, 67-68

PRAISE THE LORD, O MY SOUL

HENRY FRANCES LYTE

Praise, my soul, the King of heaven;
To his feet thy tribute bring;
Ransomed, healed, restored, forgiven,
Who like thee his praise should sing?
    Praise him, praise him,
Praise the everlasting King.

Praise him for his grace and favour
To our fathers in distress;
Praise him still the same for ever,
Slow to chide, and swift to bless;
    Praise him, praise him,
Glorious in his faithfulness.

Father-like he tends and spares us;
Well our feeble frame he knows;
In his hands he gently bears us,
Rescues us from all our foes;
    Praise him, praise him,
Widely as his mercy flows.

Angels, help us to adore him,
Ye behold him face to face;
Sun and moon, bow down before him,
Dwellers all in time and space;
    Praise him, praise him.
Praise with us the God of grace.

Now the birth of Jesus Christ was on this wise: When as his mother Mary was espoused to Joseph, before they came together, she was found with child of the Holy Ghost. Then Joseph her husband, being a just man, and not willing to make her a public example, was minded to put her away privily. But while he thought on these things, behold, the angel of the Lord appeared unto him in a dream, saying, Joseph, thou son of David, fear not to take unto thee Mary thy wife: for that which is conceived in her is of the Holy Ghost. And she shall bring forth a son, and thou shalt call his name JESUS: for he shall save his people from their sins. --- MATTHEW 1:18-21

THE VIGIL OF JOSEPH

ELSA BARKER

"Ah, what am I, that God has chosen me
To bear this blessed burden, to endure
Daily the presence of this loveliness,
To guide this Glory that shall guide the world?
Brawny these arms to win Him bread, and broad
This bosom to sustain her. But my heart
Quivers in lonely pain before that Beauty
It loves—and serves—and cannot understand!"

ANNUNCIATION TO JOACHIM. Artist Unknown. Superstock.

JOSEPH'S STORY

PAMELA KENNEDY

J oseph was a simple man living a quiet life in Nazareth. His shop was filled with the scents and sounds of carpentry. Hammers, chisels, planes, and saws hung on the walls. This afternoon, he hummed as he planed lumber for shelves. He was building furniture for the home that he would share with his bride after they were wed. Stopping for a moment, he stretched his arms and glanced at the doorway.

"Have you been standing there long?" he asked. Mary shook her head and laughed softly. He smiled at her. Despite her youth, she possessed maturity and was admired by many in Nazareth. The older women often commented that she would be a good wife. Joseph agreed, but he thought more of her beauty and the love they would share.

He beckoned her to sit beside him on the bench. He took her hands in his and smiled into her dark eyes. "Why so serious on such a sunny afternoon? Do you think these shelves won't be deep enough for your bowls and pots?"

"Joseph," she started slowly. "I have something to tell you. Something very difficult to explain."

"Ah, you want three shelves now," he teased.

"No, it's not about shelves." She looked down at their clasped hands. "Oh, Joseph, I am with child."

The words struck him like stones. He dropped her hands as if they had burned his. "What? How?" He stammered; then, with an explosive burst of realization, "Who? Who is the father?" he demanded.

Her lips trembled, but she raised her face to his and spoke with conviction. "The Spirit of God. He is the Father of my child."

Joseph jumped to his feet. "Mary, I trusted you, pledged my love to you before witnesses. You ask me to believe this?"

"But Joseph, it is true. An angel appeared. He told me that I was to be the mother of the Messiah. . . ."

"Enough!" Joseph bellowed. "Enough I say!"

Mary shielded her face with her hands. Her shoulders shook with sobs. She looked so alone, so helpless. But Joseph refused to feel pity.

"You are a simple peasant girl. What makes you think an angel would speak to you? Leave me," he said hoarsely.

The shop that had once seemed filled with golden light was now dark. Joseph grabbed a sturdy plank and slammed it onto the workbench. Long into the night, he pounded and cut, sanded and shaped, working his anger into the wood. He was tempted to drag Mary before the Sanhedrin, expose her shame, and condemn her to be stoned. Or perhaps he should divorce her publicly and doom her to the life of an outcast. In the end, he knew he loved her too much to make her suffer. He determined to divorce her quietly. Exhausted, he fell into bed and slept.

His dreams were filled with blazing light, and a voice rang through the brightness: "Joseph, thou son of David, fear not to take unto thee Mary thy wife: for that which is conceived in her is of the Holy Ghost. And she shall bring forth a son, and thou shalt call his name Jesus: for he shall save his people from their sins."

Joseph awoke in quiet darkness. The words spoken in the dream, however, were as clear as if they had been burned into the timbers overhead. In the morning, Joseph hurried to the synagogue in a state of wonder. Should he tell of his remarkable dream? Would he be laughed out of the synagogue? Lost in thought, he stood with the others as the rabbi read from the prophet Isaiah.

"The Lord himself shall give you a sign," the rabbi read. "Behold, a virgin shall conceive and bear a son, and shall call his name Immanuel."

Joseph was stunned. Mary's announcement, his dream, the prophecy. Now he understood. God had chosen to bless His people, and He had picked an innocent maid and a simple Nazarene carpenter as His instruments. Joseph excused himself and ran to Mary's home.

Together, they recounted their individual miracles, and their hearts were joined in fear and faith. They had little knowledge of the path before them, but they shared a new confidence in the One who had designed it. They knew that He alone could give them the courage to follow where He led.

Angels, from the Realms of Glory

James Montgomery

Henry Smart

An - gels, from the realms of glo - ry, Wing your flight o'er all the earth; Ye who sang cre - a - tion's sto - ry, Now pro - claim Mes - si - ah's birth: Come and wor - ship, Come and wor - ship, Wor - ship Christ, the new - born King!

Shepherds, in the fields abiding,
Watching o'er your flocks by night,
God with man is now residing;
Yonder shines the infant Light:
Come and worship,
Come and worship,
Worship Christ, the newborn King!

Sages, leave your contemplations;
Brighter visions beam afar.
Seek the great Desire of nations;
Ye have seen his natal star:
Come and worship,
Come and worship,
Worship Christ, the newborn King!

Saints, before the altar bending,
Watching long in hope and fear,
Suddenly the Lord descending,
In his temple shall appear:
Come and worship,
Come and worship,
Worship Christ, the newborn King!

Though an infant now we view him,
He shall fill his Father's throne,
Gather all the nations round him,
Every knee shall then bow down:
Come and worship,
Come and worship,
Worship Christ, the newborn King!

The First Coming

When He came, there was no light.

When He left, there was no darkness.

MARTIN LUTHER

CHAPTER FOUR

PASSAGE TO BETHLEHEM by Anton Becker. Superstock.

And it came to pass in those days, that there went out a decree from Caesar Augustus, that all the world should be taxed. (And this taxing was first made when Cyrenius was governor of Syria.) And all went to be taxed, every one into his own city. And Joseph also went up from Galilee, out of the city of Nazareth, into Judaea, unto the city of David, which is called Bethlehem; (because he was of the house and lineage of David:) To be taxed with Mary his espoused wife, being great with child. --- LUKE 2:1-5

JOSEPH

GRACE NOLL CROWELL

How weary and how tired they must have been,
Coming from Nazareth since the day's pale start,
Joseph with great responsibility,
Mary bearing earth's Saviour 'neath her heart.
Nearing the village at the set of the sun,
The man must hasten for a place to rest;
He watched the woman with grave, anxious eyes,
Seeing her clutch a white hand to her breast.

Was she too tired? Had they come too far?
Had his love failed this gentle, precious one?
And now the crowded inn, the words "No room"
For Mary soon to mother God's dear Son!
Joseph was deeply troubled. Could there be
No place in all this throng for them to go?
Then, suddenly, the stable and a hand
Bidding them enter. God had planned it so!

THE NATIVITY by Alvise Dal Friso. Christie's Images.

And so it was, that, while they were there, the days were accomplished that she should be delivered. And she brought forth her firstborn son, and wrapped him in swaddling clothes, and laid him in a manger; because there was no room for them in the inn. --- LUKE 2:6-7

A LANDLORD REMEMBERS

ELIZABETH COATSWORTH

All day my wife, the maids, the men
And I ran to and fro;
What had been done we did again,
We served both high and low.

At last we lay in weary beds,
Then boomed a staff on door,
"O Landlord, here's a desperate head!"
The inn could hold no more.

He took her to the stable near;
I woke before the day,
For with her cry our cock crowed clear,
The little ass did bray.

There seemed to come a sound of song,
I could not get to sleep,
And then the shepherds came along
And brought their bleating sheep.

That meant more runnings to and fro,
More things to eat and drink;
The work was hard, the pay was low,
We had no time to drink.

With beasts rejoicing, peering swains,
Guests calling, new-born boys,
It was enough to turn our brains
Run-running through the noise.

Then came the kings with camels, too,
And horses white as milk,
And all their gorgeous retinue
Clad in brocades and silk.

The star that troubled us by night
Had led them all the way.
We worked like mad, but it was right—
At least the kings would pay.

All's past, we've time to take our ease
And try to figure out
Why our old ox fell to his knees
And what it was about.

She looked like any maid at all
Brought to her labor here,
But there's gold buried near the wall
And the beasts still act queer.

THE ANGELS AND THE SHEPHERDS by James J. Tissot. Superstock.

And there were in the same country shepherds abiding in the field, keeping watch over their flock by night. And, lo, the angel of the Lord came upon them, and the glory of the Lord shone round about them: and they were sore afraid. --- LUKE 2:8-9

WHILE SHEPHERDS WATCHED

NAHUM TATE

While shepherds watched their flocks by night
All seated on the ground,
The angel of the Lord came down,
And glory shone around.

"Fear not," said he; (for mighty dread
Had seized their troubled mind);
"Glad tidings of great joy I bring
To you and all mankind.

"To you, in David's town, this day
Is born of David's line
A Saviour, who is Christ the Lord;
And this shall be the sign:

"The heavenly Babe you there shall find
To human view displayed,
All meanly wrapped in swathing bands,
And in a manger laid."

Thus spake the seraph; and forthwith
Appeared a shining throng
Of angels, praising God, who thus
Addressed their joyful song:

"All glory be to God on high,
And on the earth be peace;
Good-will henceforth from heaven to men
Begin and never cease."

And the angel said unto them, Fear not: for, behold, I bring you good tidings of great joy, which shall be to all people. For unto you is born this day in the city of David a Saviour, which is Christ the Lord. And this shall be a sign unto you; Ye shall find the babe wrapped in swaddling clothes, lying in a manger. --- LUKE 2:10-12

CRADLE CAROL

ELEANOR SLATER

The little birds praise you,
The wren and the sparrow,
The rabbits and squirrels
That run in the snow.
This house may be small
And this cradle be narrow.
You learned to be humble
A long time ago.

O little Lord Jesus,
Your moment is breaking.
The angels in heaven
Have polished your star.
Alone on their hillsides
The shepherds are waking.
The wise shall grow simple
And find where you are.

THE ANGEL APPEARING TO THE SHEPHERDS by Leandro Bassano. Cummer Museum of Art/Superstock.

ANGEL APPEARING TO SHEPHERDS by Nicolas Berchem. Bridgeman Art Library/Superstock.

And suddenly there was with the angel a multitude of the heavenly host praising God, and saying, Glory to God in the highest, and on earth peace, good will toward men. --- LUKE 2:13-14

CHRISTMAS HYMN

RICHARD WATSON GILDER

Tell me, what is this innumerable throng
Singing in the heavens a loud angelic song?
These are they who come with swift and shining feet
From round about the throne of God the Lord of Light to greet.

O who are these that hasten beneath the starry sky,
As if with joyful tidings that through the world shall fly?
The faithful shepherds these, who greatly were afeared
When, as they watched their flocks by night, the heavenly host appeared.

Who are these that follow across the hills of night
A star that westward hurries along the fields of light?
Three wise men from the east who myrrh and treasure bring
To lay them at the feet of him their Lord and Christ and King.

What babe new-born is this that in a manger cries?
Near on her bed of pain his happy mother lies.
O see! the air is shaken with white and heavenly wings—
This is the Lord of all the earth, this is the King of kings.

Tell me, how may I join in this holy feast
With all the kneeling world, and I of all the least?
Fear not, O faithful heart, but bring what most is meet:
Bring love alone, true love alone, and lay it at his feet.

CHRISTMAS ANGEL

PAMELA KENNEDY

Celestin knew the time was near. When the fullness of time arrived, he wanted to be ready to obey instantly. Obedience was the highest service among the angels. It was their never-ending gift to Majesty.

Celestin often pondered the way obedience seemed so difficult for humans. After all, their days were brief. Couldn't they see that Majesty knew best? He spoke His eternal wisdom to them in nature, whispered it to them through their souls, wrote it in His Word, and shouted it through His prophets. Now, in an act of grace and mercy, Majesty was sending the Only Begotten to these stiff-necked creatures. Surely now, they would finally learn obedience to their Maker's will.

It had been almost a year in earth time since Gabriel had traveled to Nazareth to speak to Mary. Celestin had watched as Gabriel told the young maiden of Majesty's plan. Despite her troubled questions, she had bowed her head in obedience and said, "I am the Lord's servant. May it be to me as you have said." How the angelic choir had rejoiced at that moment. Celestin could still hear the chords of praise echoing in the eternal reaches of heaven.

Celestin wondered how Majesty would introduce the Only Begotten. Perhaps it would be in a mighty temple with row upon row of priests praising God and blowing trumpets. Maybe there would be a tremendous earthquake or tidal wave. Celestin felt sure there would be something magnificent and wonderful for the Only Begotten.

When the call came, it was not at all what Celestin expected. He was to take a multitude of angels to a dark hillside outside a little town called Bethlehem and make an announcement to a small group of poor men tending sheep. He was to say, "Do not be afraid. I bring you good news of great joy that will be for all people. Today in the town of David a Saviour has been born to you; he is Christ the Lord. This will be a sign to you; you will find a baby wrapped in cloths and lying in a manger." Then he was to lead his fellow angels in choruses of praise to God.

"Are you sure that's it?" Celestin asked the messenger from the Throne. "No temple or palace or anything?"

The other angel shook his head. Then he raised his hand as if remembering something. "Oh, there will be a star," he added.

"A star?" Celestin repeated incredulously. "Just one star?"

"Yes," the messenger sighed, "just one star—over an animal shelter, behind an inn, on a back alley in Bethlehem."

"With all due respect," Celestin continued, "do you think you could have misunderstood? We're talking about the Only Begotten here."

The other angel looked perturbed. "That is the message as Majesty gave it to me. *I* do not question Him." Then he vanished.

Quickly, Celestin summoned a company of angels and led them to the hillside. The shepherds fell on the ground and quaked, just as Celestin had known they would. He reassured them with Majesty's words and led the angelic choir as they sang, "Glory to God in the highest, and on earth peace to men." When the angelic chorus ended and the others returned to heaven, Celestin remained behind. He wanted to see the Only Begotten.

Celestin hovered in the shadows of the tiny stable. The silver light of one star softly illuminated the walls. Mary, the obedient one, and Joseph, her husband, reclined on the straw. Mary held an infant wrapped in swaddling cloths. Could this be the Only Begotten—here, in these rude surroundings? It was unthinkable. Celestin recalled the dazzling light originating from Majesty's throne, the angels constantly in attendance, the never-ending praises. Then he gazed once more at the little family surrounded by sleeping cows and sheep.

Suddenly, a solitary word flashed into Celestin's mind: *love*. Here in this humble setting, Majesty had spoken it, not with thunder or earthquake, nor with an angelic chorus or even a trumpet blast, but with flesh and blood. The Only Begotten had left the glories of heaven to bring true love to humanity. Here in this tiny town it would begin, but Celestin knew such love could never be confined. A twinge of envy touched Celestin's heart as he realized even an angel could never know such joy as this. He bowed then in reverence before the tiny one lying in Mary's arms, and a gentle breeze brushed the Baby's cheek as the angel whispered, "Holy, Holy, Holy."

Whence Comes This Rush of Wings

TRADITIONAL FRENCH   TRADITIONAL FRENCH

Whence comes this rush of wings a - far,

Fol - low - ing straight the No - el star?

Birds from the woods in won - drous flight,

Beth - le - hem seek this Ho - ly Night.

ANNUNCIATION (detail) by Simon Vouet. Pushkin Museum of Fine Arts/Superstock.

"Tell us, ye birds, why come ye here,
Into this stable, poor and drear?"
"Hastening we seek the newborn King,
And all our sweetest music bring."

Hark how the Greenfinch bears his part,
Philomel, too, with tender heart,
Chants from her leafy, dark retreat
Re, mi, fa, sol, in accents sweet.

Angels and shepherds, birds of the sky,
Come where the Son of God doth lie;
Christ on the earth with man doth dwell,
Join in the shout, Noel, Noel.

And it came to pass, as the angels were gone away from them into heaven, the shepherds said one to another, Let us now go even unto Bethlehem, and see this thing which is come to pass, which the Lord hath made known unto us. --- LUKE 2:15

THE SHEPHERDS

SAMUEL TAYLOR COLERIDGE

The shepherds went their hasty way
And found the lowly stable shed
Where the virgin mother lay;
And now they checked their eager tread,
For to the babe, that at her bosom clung,
A mother's song the virgin mother sung.

They told her how a glorious light,
Streaming from a heavenly throng,
Around them shone, suspending night,
While, sweeter than a mother's song,
Blest angels heralded the Saviour's birth:
Glory to God on high! and peace on earth.

She listened to the tale divine,
And closer still the babe she pressed;
And while she cried, "The babe is mine!"
The milk rushed faster to her breast:
Joy rose within her, like a summer's morn:
Peace, peace on earth! the Prince of peace is born.

ADORATION OF THE SHEPHERDS by Jan Cossiers. Superstock.

ADORATION OF THE SHEPHERDS by Domenico Zampieri Domenichino. Fine Art Photographic Library.

And they came with haste, and found Mary, and Joseph, and the babe lying in a manger. And when they had seen it, they made known abroad the saying which was told them concerning this child. And all they that heard it wondered at those things which were told them by the shepherds. --- LUKE 2:16-18

A CRADLE SONG

PADRAIC COLUM

O men from the fields!
Come gently within.
Tread softly, softly,
O! men coming in.

Mavourneen is going
From me and from you,
Where Mary will fold him
With mantle of blue!

From reek of the smoke
And cold of the floor,
And the peering of things
Across the half-door.

O men from the fields!
Soft, softly come through—
Mary puts round him
Her mantle of blue.

But Mary kept all these things, and pondered them in her heart. And the shepherds returned, glorifying and praising God for all the things that they had heard and seen, as it was told unto them. --- LUKE 2:19-20

PONDERINGS

MARGARET RORKE

Did she, His mother, reminisce,
And did it go a bit like this?
"Just as my time was 'bout to be,
My husband said by some decree
We had to go, so he'd been told,
To Bethlehem to be enrolled.
It was a dirty, weary ride,
And Joseph walked it by my side.
When we arrived among his kin,
There was no lodging at the inn.
But in compassion someone gave
Directions to a little cave,
And in that shelter so forlorn
My little baby boy was born.

So sweet and gentle right from birth!
And yet I knew He'd change the earth.
I had been told He was God's Son,
And, as His life was just begun,
Above us shone a holy star
That drew three wise men from afar.
From hills nearby the shepherds came
And called my baby by His name.
They said that angels had appeared
And calmed the ones who plainly feared
By telling them of peace, good will:
A prophecy that He'd fulfill.
All this had set my child apart.
These things I've pondered in my heart."

MADONNA AND CHILD by Bartolomé Esteban Murillo. Staatliche Kunstsammlungen/Superstock.

THE HOLY FAMILY by Raphael. Superstock.

And when eight days were accomplished for the circumcising of the child, his name was called JESUS, which was so named of the angel before he was conceived in the womb. --- LUKE 2:21

CHRISTMAS

Saint Augustine of Hippo

Maker of the sun,
He is made under the sun.
In the Father he remains,
From his mother he goes forth.

Creator of heaven and earth,
He was born on earth under heaven.
Unspeakably wise,
He is wisely speechless.

Filling the world,
He lies in a manger.
Ruler of the stars,
He nurses at his mother's bosom.

He is both great in the nature of God,
And small in the form of a servant.

THERE'S SOMETHING ABOUT THAT NAME

William J. Gaither

Jesus, Jesus, Jesus;
There's just something about that name.
Master, Savior, Jesus,
Like the fragrance after the rain;

Jesus, Jesus, Jesus,
Let all Heaven and earth proclaim;
Kings and kingdoms will all pass away,
But there's something about that name.

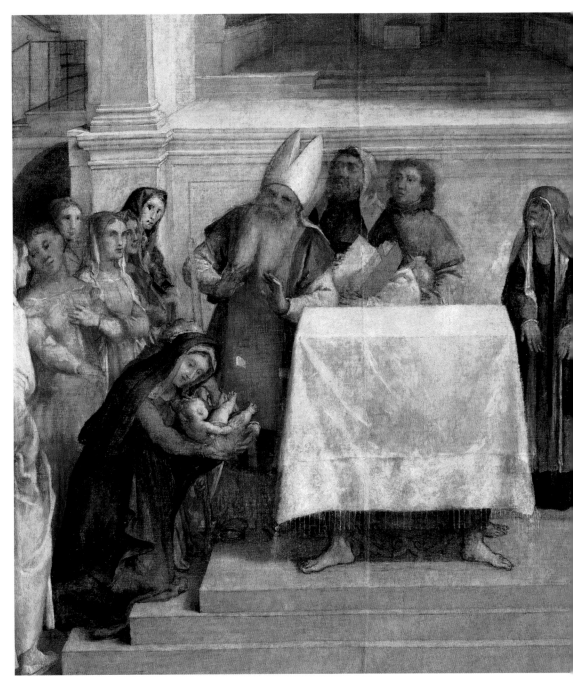

THE PRESENTATION IN THE TEMPLE by Lorenzo Lotto. Erich Lessing/Art Resource.

And behold, there was a man in Jerusalem, whose name was Simeon; and the same man was just and devout, waiting for the consolation of Israel: and the Holy Ghost was upon him. And it was revealed unto him by the Holy Ghost, that he should not see death, before he had seen the Lord's Christ. --- LUKE 2:25-26

THE PRINCE OF PEACE

PHILLIP DODDRIDGE

Hark! the glad sound! the Saviour comes,
The Saviour promised long:
Let every heart prepare a throne,
And every voice a song.

He comes, the broken heart to bind,
The bleeding soul to cure,
And with the treasures of His grace
To enrich the humble poor.

Our glad hosannas, Prince of Peace,
Thy welcome shall proclaim,
And Heaven's eternal arches ring
With Thy beloved name.

And he came by the Spirit into the temple: and when the parents brought in the child Jesus, to do for him after the custom of the law, Then took he him up in his arms, and blessed God, and said, Lord, now lettest thou thy servant depart in peace, according to thy word: For mine eyes have seen thy salvation. --- LUKE 2:27-30

CHRIST'S NATIVITY

HENRY VAUGHAN

Awake, glad heart! get up and sing!
It is the birthday of thy King.
    Awake! awake!
    The sun doth shake
Light from his locks, and all the way
Breathing perfumes, doth spice the day.

Awake, awake! hark how th' wood rings;
Winds whisper, and the busy springs
    A concert make;

    Awake! awake!
Man is their high-priest, and should rise
To offer up the sacrifice.

I would I were some bird, or star,
Flutt'ring in woods, or lifted far
    Above this inn
    And road of sin!
Then either star or bird should be
Shining or singing still to thee.

THE PRESENTATION AT THE TEMPLE by Sebastien Bourdon. Musee du Louvre/Superstock.

The World Worships

If I were a shepherd, I would bring a lamb.

If I were a wise man, I would do my part;

Yet what can I give Him—Give my heart.

CHRISTINA GEORGINA ROSSETTI

CHAPTER FIVE

Now when Jesus was born in Bethlehem of Judaea in the days of Herod the king, behold, there came wise men from the east to Jerusalem, Saying, Where is he that is born King of the Jews? for we have seen his star in the east, and are come to worship him. --- MATTHEW 2:1-2

BRIGHTEST AND BEST OF THE SONS OF THE MORNING

REGINALD HEBER

Brightest and best of the sons of the morning,
Dawn on our darkness, and lend us Thine aid!
Star of the east, the horizon adorning,
Guide where our infant Redeemer is laid!

Cold on His cradle the dewdrops are shining;
Low lies His head with the beasts of the stall;
Angels adore Him in slumber reclining,
Maker and Monarch and Saviour of all.

Brightest and best of the sons of the morning,
Dawn on our darkness, and lend us Thine aid!
Star of the east, the horizon adorning,
Guide where our infant Redeemer is laid!

THE JOURNEY OF THE MAGI by Stefano di Giovanni Sassetta. Superstock.

THE WISE AND HEROD by James J. Tissot. Superstock.

When Herod the king had heard these things, he was troubled, and all Jerusalem with him. And when he had gathered all the chief priests and scribes of the people together, he demanded of them where Christ should be born. --- MATTHEW 2:3-4

THAT HOLY THING

GEORGE MACDONALD

They were all looking for a king
To slay their foes and lift them high;
Thou cam'st, a little baby thing
That made a woman cry.

O Son of Man, to right my lot
Naught but Thy presence can avail;
Yet on the road Thy wheels are not,
Nor on the sea Thy sail!

My how or when Thou wilt not heed,
But come down Thine own secret stair,
That Thou mayst answer all my need—
Yea, every bygone prayer.

And they said unto him, In Bethlehem of Judaea: for thus it is written by the prophet, And thou Bethlehem, in the land of Juda, art not the least among the princes of Juda: for out of thee shall come a Governor, that shall rule my people Israel. --- MATTHEW 2:5-6

BETHLEHEM OF JUDEA

JESSIE WILMORE MURTON

O little town of Bethlehem, beside the blue hills sleeping,
I wonder if you dream tonight? And what your dream may be?
Is it of gray, old shepherds with white flocks in their keeping,
And two lone, weary pilgrims come down from Galilee?
Do strains of angel music, from angels' fingers sweeping
Across their golden harp strings, stir again in memory?

O little town of Bethlehem, beside the blue hills dreaming,
I wonder if you muse on how that glorious anthem rolled
Across the silent valley? How fell the strange star's beaming
Upon drowsy cattle, and touched the hay with gold?
And how a hint of radiance above a small head gleaming
Filled Mary's heart with wonder, and yet with fear untold?

O little town of Bethlehem, beside the blue hills nodding,
Though centuries have left you still dreaming as of yore,
The shepherds' plain, the herdsmen their placid cattle prodding,
The ancient landmarks standing, untroubled as before;
Yet hearts of many peoples, the light feet and the plodding
Have made of you, O Bethlehem, a shrine, forevermore!

CANA - VIEW OF SUNSET by David Roberts. Newberry Library/Superstock.

ADORATION OF THE MAGI AT BETHLEHEM by Benozzo Gozzoli. Scala/Art Resource.

Then Herod, when he had privily called the wise men, inquired of them diligently what time the star appeared. And he sent them to Bethlehem, and said, Go and search diligently for the young child; and when ye have found him, bring me word again, that I may come and worship him also. --- MATTHEW 2:7-8

HOW FAR TO BETHLEHEM

MADELEINE SWEENY MILLER

"How far is it to Bethlehem town?"
Just over Jerusalem hills adown,
Past lovely Rachel's white-domed tomb—
Sweet shrine of motherhood's young doom.

It isn't far to Bethlehem town—
Just over the dusty roads adown,
Past Wise Men's well, still offering
Cool draughts from welcome wayside spring;
Past shepherds with their flutes of reed
That charm the woolly sheep they lead;
Past boys with kites on hilltops flying,
And soon you're there where Bethlehem's lying.
Sunned white and sweet on olived slopes,
Gold-lighted still with Judah's hopes.

And so we find the Shepherd's field
And plain that gave rich Boaz yield
And look where Herod's villa stood.
We thrill that earthly parenthood
Could foster Christ who was all-good;
And thrill that Bethlehem town today
Looks down on Christian homes that pray.

It isn't far to Bethlehem town!
It's anywhere that Christ comes down
And finds in people's friendly face
A welcome and abiding place.
The road to Bethlehem runs right through
The homes of folks like me and you.

When they had heard the king, they departed; and, lo, the star, which they saw in the east, went before them, till it came and stood over where the young child was. When they saw the star, they rejoiced with exceeding great joy. --- MATTHEW 2:9-10

THE CHRISTMAS STAR

NANCY BYRD TURNER

High in the heavens a single star,
Of pure, imperishable light;
Out on the desert strange and far
Dim riders riding through the night:
Above a hilltop sudden song
Like silver trumpets down the sky—
And all to welcome One so young
He scarce could lift a cry!

Stars rise and set, that star shines on:
Songs fail, but still that music beats
Through all the ages come and gone,
In lane and field and city streets.
And we who catch the Christmas gleam,
Watching with children on the hill,
We know, we know it is no dream—
He stands among us still!

THE WISE MEN JOURNEYING TO BETHLEHEM by James J. Tissot. Jewish Museum/Superstock.

THE ADORATION OF THE MAGI by Hendrick De Clerck. Christie's Images.

And when they were come into the house, they saw the young child with Mary his mother, and fell down, and worshipped him. --- MATTHEW 2:11A

THREE WISE MEN JOURNEYED

ALONZO NEWTON BENN

Three wise men journeyed eastward,
Their hearts were full of love,
And on and on they hurried,
Led by the star above
That shone high o'er the manger
Wherein the Christ Child lay
With Mary, virgin mother,
That far off Christmas day.

When Bethlehem they entered
And found the new born King,
They knelt beside the manger,
And gifts that they did bring

Bestowed they on the Infant
To prove their love was true—
Their love should be a guidance
Each day for me and you.

So let us meet together
This blessed Christmas day,
And glorify our Saviour
With sweetest roundelay;
Forgetting all our troubles,
And with much joy let's sing
That Christ is our Redeemer,
Our Saviour and our King.

ADORATION OF THE MAGI by Antonio Allegri Correggio. Scala/Art Resource.

And when they had opened their treasures, they presented unto him gifts; gold, and frankincense, and myrrh. --- MATTHEW 2:11B

THE THREE KINGS

HENRY WADSWORTH LONGFELLOW

Three Kings came riding from far away,
Melchior and Gaspar and Balthazar;
Three Wise Men out of the East were they,
And they traveled by night and they slept by day,
For their guide was a beautiful, wonderful star.

The star was so beautiful, large and clear,
That all the other stars of the sky
Became a white mist in the atmosphere;
And by this they knew that the coming was near
Of the Prince foretold in the prophecy.

Three caskets they bore on their saddle-bows,
Three caskets of gold with golden keys;
Their robes were of crimson silk, with rows
Of bells and pomegranates and fur below,
Their turbans like blossoming almond-trees.

And so the Three Kings rode into the West,
Through the dusk of night over hill and dell,
And sometimes they nodded with beard on breast,
And sometimes talked, as they paused to rest,
With the people they met at some wayside well.

And when they came to Jerusalem,
Herod the Great, who had heard this thing,
Sent for the Wise Men and questioned them;
And said, "Go down unto Bethlehem,
And bring me tidings of this new king."

So they rode away, and the star stood still,
The only one in the gray of morn;
Yes, it stopped, it stood still of its own free will,
Right over Bethlehem on the hill,
The city of David where Christ was born.

And cradled there in the scented hay,
In the air made sweet by the breath of kine,
The little Child in the manger lay,
The Child that would be King one day
Of a kingdom not human, but divine.

They laid their offerings at his feet:
The gold was their tribute to a King;
The frankincense, with its odor sweet,
Was for the Priest, the Paraclete;
The myrrh for the body's burying.

And the mother wondered and bowed her head,
And sat as still as a statue of stone;
Her heart was troubled yet comforted,
Remembering what the angel had said
Of an endless reign and of David's throne.

Then the Kings rode out of the city gate,
With a clatter of hoofs in proud array;
But they went not back to Herod the Great,
For they knew his malice and feared his hate,
And returned to their homes by another way.

We Three Kings
of Orient Are

John Henry Hopkins Jr.   John Henry Hopkins Jr.

We three kings of O - ri - ent are, bear - ing gifts we

tra - verse a - far, field and foun - tain, moor and moun - tain,

fol - low - ing yon - der star. O star of won - der,

star of night, star with roy - al beau - ty bright, west - ward

lead - ing, still pro - ceed - ing, guide us to thy per - fect light.

Born a King on Bethlehem's plain,
Gold I bring to crown him again,
King forever, ceasing never,
Over us all to reign.
Star of wonder, star of night,
Star with royal beauty bright,
Westward leading, still proceeding,
Guide us to thy perfect light.

Frankincense to offer have I;
Incense owns a Deity nigh;
Prayer and praising, all men raising,
Worship him God most high.
Star of wonder, star of night,
Star with royal beauty bright,
Westward leading, still proceeding,
Guide us to thy perfect light.

Myrrh is mine; its bitter perfume
Breathes a life of gathering gloom:
Sorrowing, sighing, bleeding, dying,
Sealed in the stone cold tomb.
Star of wonder, star of night,
Star with royal beauty bright,
Westward leading, still proceeding,
Guide us to thy perfect light.

Glorious now behold him arise,
King and God and Sacrifice.
Alleluia, Alleluia,
Earth to heaven replies.
Star of wonder, star of night,
Star with royal beauty bright,
Westward leading, still proceeding,
Guide us to thy perfect light.

JOSEPH'S DREAM by Luca Giordano. Erich Lessing/Art Resource.

And being warned of God in a dream that they should not return to Herod, they departed into their own country another way. And when they were departed, behold, the angel of the Lord appeareth to Joseph in a dream, saying, Arise, and take the young child and his mother, and flee into Egypt, and be thou there until I bring thee word: for Herod will seek the young child to destroy him. --- MATTHEW 2:12-13

FLIGHT INTO EGYPT

JOHNIELU BARBER BRADFORD

He called her Mary, who rode on my back;
She called him Joseph, who walked by my side;
His hand was easy and his voice was soft
And he walked with patience, love, and pride.

I was their beast, yet I sensed their plight;
I heard them talk and plan and pray.
I knew the dream the angel brought,
And I shared their faith along the way.

But the load I carried, a mother and Child,
Rode as light as the touch that guided me;
And my master, Joseph, who walked by my side
Was as kind and gentle as a man could be.

REST ON THE FLIGHT INTO
EGYPT by Jean-Honore Fragonard.
Christie's Images.

When he arose, he took the young child and his mother by night, and departed into Egypt: And was there until the death of Herod: that it might be fulfilled which was spoken of the Lord by the prophet, saying, Out of Egypt have I called my son. --- MATTHEW 2:14-15

OUT OF EGYPT HAVE I CALLED MY SON

CAROLINE HAZARD

The mighty river flows as when Thine eyes,
Thy baby eyes, in wonder saw it flow.
The Pyramids stand there; no one may know
Their countless years, or ancient builders wise;
Thy childish gaze was caught in glad surprise
To see the haughty camels come and go;
The ass thy mother rode still ambles slow;

Unmoved by centuries the country lies.
Up from the calm, the peace, the mystic land,
Back to the scene of conflict and of strife,
Thy parents journeyed at the Lord's command.
A touch of glory rests upon the place
Which gave its shelter to Thine infant grace
And nourished Thee to be the Life of Life.

THE SECOND CHRISTMAS

PAMELA KENNEDY

M ary looked up from the muddy water at the river's edge and watched, smiling, as her young son struggled to keep his balance. His chubby legs wobbled and his dimpled arms beat at the air as he strained to take each step. She laughed aloud as the little boy finally lost his balance and plopped down on the dusty path. For a moment he looked as though he might cry, but then a bright orange poppy caught his eye. He crawled over to examine it more closely.

Mary turned back to her washing, dunking and squeezing it rhythmically in the flowing stream. Soon Jesus toddled back to the water and sat down awkwardly next to her.

"And what are you about today, my little one?" Mary asked the wide-eyed child. Giggling in reply, he splashed his bare toes in the lapping water and tossed handfuls of sand into the air.

Mary wrung out the clothes and tossed them into a basket, then sat down to rest for a moment beside the stream. She studied her son as he played, his dark curls bouncing with each movement.

Tomorrow her little Jesus would be a year old. How different, she thought, this year would be from the last. Since then the little family of three had fled from their homeland into the unfamiliarity of Egypt. Mary wondered how long their stay would be. She yearned for the faces of her family. She longed to show them her firstborn son, to hear them praise his beauty and his infant accomplishments. She sighed, lost in her thoughts.

Sensing his mother's unrest, the little boy nestled against her. Pulling himself up by her sleeve, he placed a grubby hand against his mother's cheek. Instinctively, Mary took the child in her arms, loosened her garment, and began to nurse him. As he settled against her, she hummed a quiet lullaby.

Her mind still had trouble reconciling all the contradictions of this little one. He was the Son of God, yet he depended on her for life. He was a miracle, yet so like any other child. He looked as others did, but he carried the beauty of holiness within him. How could this little hand, now so tightly curled around her fingers, have formed mankind? She studied the tiny lips that could not yet speak a word. How could they have ordered the universe into being, separated light from darkness and sea from land?

SUR LE NIL by Hermann David Soloman. Christie's Images.

Satisfied, the child wriggled around in his mother's lap and babbled in contentment. Mary began to sing the song placed in her heart when the angel visited her almost two years earlier.

The baby grew still and listened quietly to her clear voice mingling with the soft Egyptian breeze: "My soul doth magnify the Lord . . ."

As she sang, a strange thing began to happen. A look of comprehension began to fill the baby's dark eyes. His expression became intent, and his tiny mouth smiled.

When the song was finished, the two of them sat silently, caught up in a unique design of love—a love of mother and son, both human and divine, temporal and eternal. Then Mary quickly leaned and kissed the boy. He laughed and returned her kiss with a hug. Swinging him onto her hip, she balanced the laundry with her free arm and stood. Slowly she started up the path to their village.

This year there would be no adoring shepherds or angel choirs; no blazing star would mark the passage of her son's first year. For now he was just another child, cherished just as any other. Her heart could not look beyond that now.

"Blessed birthday, Jesus," she whispered, and he clapped his chubby hands with glee.

FLIGHT INTO EGYPT by Hans Thoma. Superstock.

But when Herod was dead, behold, an angel of the Lord appeareth in a dream to Joseph in Egypt, Saying, Arise, and take the young child and his mother, and go into the land of Israel: for they are dead which sought the young child's life. And he arose, and took the young child and his mother, and came into the land of Israel. . . . And he came and dwelt in a city called Nazareth: that it might be fulfilled which was spoken by the prophets, He shall be called a Nazarene.

--- MATTHEW 2:19-21, 23

HOME TO NAZARETH

GRACE NOLL CROWELL

Coarse, harsh cloth for His swaddling clothes,
And rough-stemmed hay for the Christ Child's bed,
And the only lamp, a star that shone
Through the rafters overhead.

But Mary pillowed the little form
On an arm as soft as a white dove's breast,
And she shaped the hay with her gentle hands
Into a soft, downy nest.

And she thought of a room in Nazareth,
Of a white bed under the eaves of sod—
Strange that she should have given birth
Here to the Son of God.

Strange these coarse, harsh swaddling clothes
On the tender flesh of her little One,

When there were robes in a cedar chest,
Cedar from Lebanon.

"I will take Thee home, my little Son,"
Mary, the beautiful mother, said,
"I will take Thee home to my small, clean room,
Home to a soft, clean bed.

"And I will open a fragrant chest,
Which Joseph, Thy father, hath made—
In it are fine, twilled linen slips,
And a woolly coat is laid.

"Fine, twilled linen from silver flax,
And fleecy wool from a snow-white sheep—
Yea, we will go home through the starry dusk.
Sleep, my little One, sleep."

Now his parents went to Jerusalem every year at the feast of the passover. And when he was twelve years old, they went up to Jerusalem after the custom of the feast. And when they had fulfilled the days, as they returned, the child Jesus tarried behind in Jerusalem; and Joseph and his mother knew not of it. But they, supposing him to have been in the company, went a day's journey; and they sought him among their kinsfolk and acquaintance. And when they found him not, they turned back again to Jerusalem, seeking him. --- LUKE 2:41-45

FROM THE TWELFTH CHRISTMAS

ONA JANE MEENS

Softly the twilight had fallen,
The stars appeared one by one,
While on a carpenter's doorstep
Sat a mother and her son.

Her mind was filled with memories
As she watched the fading light;
Many mysteries in her life
Were casting shadows tonight.

A sense of foreboding disturbed her
As she drew the boy to her side.

"My son, I wish you could always
In safety with me abide."

Twelve wonderful years of his life
His mother had kept him her own,
Hiding the mystery in her heart,
His mission as she had known.

But tonight, her heart understood;
Sands of time had quickly run;
For now she must give back to God
This wonderful gift—His Son.

JERUSALEM FROM THE MOUNT OF OLIVES by Gustav Bauernfeind. Christie's Images/Superstock.

And it came to pass, that after three days they found him in the temple, sitting in the midst of the doctors, both hearing them, and asking them questions. And all that heard him were astonished at his understanding and answers. And when they saw him . . . his mother said unto him, Son, why hast thou thus dealt with us? behold, thy father and I have sought thee sorrowing. And he said unto them, How is it that ye sought me? wist ye not that I must be about my Father's business? . . . And he went down with them, and came to Nazareth, and was subject unto them . . . And Jesus increased in wisdom and stature, and in favour with God and man. --- LUKE 2:46-49, 51-52

FROM THE TWELFTH CHRISTMAS

ONA JANE MEENS

"I must do my Father's bidding;
Today I am twelve years old,
And He will make it plain to me,
So His plan I can unfold.
I will give the world His message,
That all men may understand
That I have come from the Father
To reveal His love for man."

The lad alone on the doorstep,
Awaiting the cool, gray dawn;
In His heart He heard the angels
Singing their marvelous song.
And His Father's voice from heaven
Borne to him by the breeze:
"Thou art My own beloved Son,
In Thee I am well pleased."

JESUS FOUND IN THE TEMPLE by Carl Heinrich Bloch. Frederiksborg Castle Church/Superstock.

The Lord Is King

Jesus Christ will be Lord of all or
He will not be Lord at all.

SAINT AUGUSTINE OF HIPPO

CHAPTER SIX

Rejoice greatly, O daughter of Zion; shout, O daughter of Jerusalem: behold, thy King cometh unto thee: he is just, and having salvation; lowly, and riding upon an ass, and upon a colt the foal of an ass. . . . He shall feed his flock like a shepherd: he shall gather the lambs with his arm, and carry them in his bosom, and shall gently lead those that are with young. --- ZECHARIAH 9:9, ISAIAH 40:11

THE SHEPHERD SPEAKS

JOHN ERSKINE

Out of the midnight sky a great dawn broke,
And a voice singing flooded us with song.
In David's city was He born, it sang,
A Saviour, Christ the Lord. Then while I sat
Shivering with the thrill of that great cry,
A mighty choir a thousandfold more sweet
Suddenly sang, Glory to God, and Peace—
Peace on the earth; my heart, almost unnerved
By that swift loveliness, would hardly beat.
Speechless we waited till the accustomed night
Gave us no promise more of sweet surprise;
Then scrambling to our feet, without a word
We started through the fields to find the Child.

THE ADORATION OF THE SHEPHERDS by Christian W.E. Dietrich. A.K.G./Superstock.

ADORATION OF THE MAGI by Diego Rodriguez Velazquez. Museo del Prado/Superstock.

Come unto me, all ye that labour and are heavy laden, and I will give you rest. Take my yoke upon you, and learn of me; for I am meek and lowly in heart: and ye shall find rest unto your souls. For my yoke is easy, and my burden is light. --- MATTHEW 11:28-30

THE KINGS OF THE EAST

KATHARINE LEE BATES

The Kings of the East are riding
Tonight to Bethlehem.
The sunset glows dividing,
The Kings of the East are riding;
A star their journey guiding,
Gleaming with gold and gem.
The Kings of the East are riding
Tonight to Bethlehem.

To a strange, sweet harp of Zion
The starry host troops forth;
The golden glaived Orion
To a strange sweet harp of Zion;

The Archer and the Lion,
The watcher of the North.
To a strange sweet harp of Zion
The starry host troops forth.

There beams above a manger
The child-face of a star;
Amid the stars a stranger,
It beams above a manger;
What means this ether-ranger
To pause where poor folk are?
There beams above a manger
The child-face of a star.

For he shall grow up before him as a tender plant, and as a root out of a dry ground: he hath no form nor comeliness; and when we shall see him, there is no beauty that we should desire him. He is despised and rejected of men; a man of sorrows, and acquainted with grief: and we hid as it were our faces from him; he was despised, and we esteemed him not. --- ISAIAH 53:2-3

CHRISTMAS MORNING

ELIZABETH MADOX ROBERTS

If Bethlehem were here today,
Or this were very long ago,
There wouldn't be a winter time
Nor any cold or snow.
I'd run out through the garden gate,
And down along the pasture walk;
And off beside the cattle barns
I'd hear a kind of gentle talk.

I'd move the heavy iron chain
And pull away the wooden pin;
I'd push the door a little bit
And tiptoe very softly in.
The pigeons and the yellow hens
And all the cows would stand away;
Their eyes would open wide to see
A lady in the manger hay,

If this were very long ago
And Bethlehem were here today.
And Mother held my hand and smiled—

I mean the lady would—and she
Would take the woolly blankets off
Her little boy so I could see.

His shut-up eyes would be asleep,
And he would look just like our John,
And he would be all crumpled too,
And have a pinkish color on.
I'd watch his breath go in and out.
His little clothes would all be white.
I'd slip my finger in his hand
To feel how he could hold it tight.

And she would smile and say, "Take care,"
The mother, Mary, would, "Take care";
And I would kiss his little hand
And touch his hair.
While Mary put the blankets back
The gentle talk would soon begin.
And when I'd tiptoe softly out
I'd meet the wise men going in.

NATIVITY by Federico Barocci. Scala/Art Resource.

Surely he hath borne our griefs, and carried our sorrows: yet we did esteem him stricken, smitten of God, and afflicted. But he was wounded for our transgressions, he was bruised for our iniquities: the chastisement of our peace was upon him; and with his stripes we are healed. All we like sheep have gone astray; we have turned every one to his own way; and the LORD hath laid on him the iniquity of us all. --- ISAIAH 53:4-6

CHRIST CHILD

HENRY TREECE

Warm as a little mouse he lay,
Hay kept him from the Winter's harm;
Bleating of puzzled lamb he heard,
And voices from the near-by farm.

His mother's eyes were bent on him
As to her frozen breast he clung;
His father stopped the draughty cracks
And sang a merry herding song.

Who would have thought upon that hour
Those little hands might stay a plague,
Those eyes would quell a multitude,
That voice would still a rising wave?

Only the omens of the night,
The lowing ox, the moaning tree,
Hinted the cruelty to come:
A raven croaked, "Gethsemane!"

ADORATION OF THE SHEPHERDS by Jacob Jordaens. Superstock.

Madonna del Seggiola by Raphael. H. Armstrong Roberts.

All they that see me laugh me to scorn: they shoot out the lip, they shake the head, saying, He trusted on the LORD that he would deliver him: let him deliver him, seeing he delighted in him. But thou art he that took me out of the womb: thou didst make me hope when I was upon my mother's breasts. I was cast upon thee from the womb: thou art my God. --- PSALM 22:7-10

THE CHILD JESUS

FRANCIS QUARLES

Hail, blessed Virgin, full of heavenly grace,
Blest above all that sprang from human race;
Whose heaven-saluted womb brought forth in one
A blessed Saviour, and a blessed son:
O! what a ravishment 't had been to see
Thy little Saviour perking on thy knee!
To see him nuzzle in thy virgin breast!
His little body all unclad, undrest;
To see thy busy fingers clothe and wrap
His spradling limbs in thy indulgent lap!
To see his desperate eyes, with childish grace,
Smiling upon his smiling mother's face!
And, when his forward strength began to bloom,
To see him diddle up and down the room!
O, who would think so sweet a babe as this
Should e'er be slain by a false-hearted kiss!

THE APPARITION OF THE ANGEL TO THE SHEPHERDS by Jacopo Bassano. Sevastopol Art Museum/Superstock.

Be not far from me; for trouble is near; for there is none to help. . . . I am poured out like water, and all my bones are out of joint: my heart is like wax . . . My strength is dried up . . . and thou hast brought me into the dust of death. . . . they pierced my hands and my feet. . . . They part my garments among them, and cast lots upon my vesture. --- PSALM 22:11, 14-16, 18

SONGS OF JESUS

LOUIS F. BENSON

O sing a song of Bethlehem,
Of shepherds watching there,
And of the news that came to them
From angels in the air:
The light that shone on Bethlehem
Fills all the world today;
Of Jesus' birth and peace on earth
The angels sing alway.

O sing a song of Calvary,
Its glory and dismay;
Of Him who hung upon the Tree
And took our sins away;
For He who died on Calvary
Is risen from the grave,
And Christ, our Lord, by heaven adored,
Is mighty now to save.

FROM THE OTHER WISE MAN

HENRY VAN DYKE

Three-and-thirty years of the life of Artaban had passed away, and he was still a pilgrim, and a seeker after light. His hair, once darker than the cliffs of Zagros, was now white as the wintry snow that covered them. His eyes, that once flashed like flames of fire, were dull as embers smouldering among the ashes.

Worn and weary and ready to die, but still looking for the King, he had come for the last time to Jerusalem. He had often visited the holy city before, and had searched through all its lanes and crowded hovels and black prisons without finding any trace of the family of Nazarenes who had fled from Bethlehem long ago. But now it seemed as if he must make one more effort, and something whispered in his heart that, at last, he might succeed.

It was the season of the Passover. The city was thronged with strangers. The children of Israel, scattered in far lands all over the world, had returned to the Temple for the great feast, and there had been a confusion of tongues in the narrow streets for many days.

But on this day there was a singular agitation visible in the multitude. The sky was veiled with a portentous gloom, and currents of excitement seemed to flash through the crowd like the thrill which shakes the forest on the eve of the storm. A secret tide was sweeping them all one way. The clatter of sandals, and the soft, thick sound of thousands of bare feet shuffling over the stones, flowed unceasingly along the street that leads to the Damascus gate.

Artaban joined company with a group of people from his own country, Parthian Jews who had come up to keep the Passover, and inquired of them the cause of the tumult, and where they were going.

"We are going," they answered, "to the place called Golgotha, outside the city walls, where there is to be an execution. Have you not heard what has happened? Two famous robbers are to be crucified, and with them another, called Jesus of Nazareth, a man who has done many wonderful works among the people, so that they love him greatly. But the priests and elders have said that he must die, because he gave himself out to be the Son of God. And Pilate has sent him to the cross because he said that he was the 'King of the Jews.'"

How strangely these familiar words fell upon the tired heart of Artaban! They had led him for a lifetime over land and sea. And now they came to him darkly and mysteriously like a message of despair. The King had arisen, but He had been denied and cast out. He was about to perish. Perhaps He was already dying. Could it be the same one who had been born in Bethlehem thirty-three years ago, at whose birth the star had appeared in heaven, and of whose coming the prophets had spoken?

Artaban's heart beat unsteadily with that troubled, doubtful apprehension which is the excitement of old age. But he said within himself: "The ways of God are stranger than the thoughts of men, and it may be that I shall find the King, at last, in the hands of His enemies, and shall come in time to offer my pearl for His ransom before He dies."

So the old man followed the multitude with slow and painful steps toward the Damascus gate of the city. Just beyond the entrance of the guardhouse a troop of Macedonian soldiers came down the street, dragging a young girl with torn dress and dishevelled hair. As the Magian paused to look at her with compassion, she broke suddenly from the hands of her tormentors and threw herself at his feet, clasping him around the knees. She had seen his white cap and the winged circle on his breast.

"Have pity on me," she cried, "and save me, for the sake of the God of purity! I also am a daughter of the true religion which is taught by the Magi. My father was a merchant of Parthia, but he is dead, and I am seized for his debts to be sold as a slave. Save me from worse than death."

Artaban trembled. It was the old conflict in his soul, which had come to him in the palm-grove of Babylon and in the cottage at Bethlehem—the conflict between the expectation of faith and the impulse of love. Twice the gift which he had consecrated to the worship of religion had been drawn from his hand to the service of humanity. This was the third trial, the ultimate probation, the final and irrevocable choice.

Was it his great opportunity or his last temptation? He could not tell. One thing only was clear in the darkness of his mind—it was inevitable. And does not the inevitable come from God?

One thing only was sure to his divided heart—to rescue this helpless girl would be a true deed of love. And is not love the light of the soul?

He took the pearl from his bosom. Never had it seemed so luminous, so radiant, so full of tender, living lustre. He laid it in the hand of the slave.

"This is thy ransom, daughter! It is the last of my treasures which I kept for the King."

THE ADORATION OF THE MAGI by Giovanni Battista Paggi. Christie's Images.

While he spoke, the darkness of the sky thickened, and shuddering tremors ran through the earth, heaving convulsively like the breast of one who struggles with mighty grief.

The walls of the houses rocked to and fro. Stones were loosened and crashed into the street. Dust clouds filled the air. The soldiers fled in terror, reeling like drunken men. But Artaban and the girl whom he had ransomed crouched helpless beneath the wall of the Praetorium.

What had he to fear? What had he to live for? He had given away the last remnant of his tribute for the King. He had parted with the last hope of finding Him. The quest was over, and it had failed. But even in that thought, accepted and embraced, there was peace. It was not resignation. It was not submission. It was something more profound and searching. He knew that all was well, because he had done the best that he could, from day to day. He had been true to the light that had been given to him. He had looked for more. And if he had not found it, if a failure was all that came out of his life, doubt-less that was the best that was possible. He had not seen the revelation of "life everlasting, incorruptible and immortal." But he knew that even if he could live his earthly life over again, it could not be otherwise than it had been.

One more lingering pulsation of the earthquake quivered through the ground. A heavy tile, shaken from the roof, fell and struck the old man on the temple. He lay breathless and pale, with his gray head resting on the young girl's shoulder, and the blood trickling from the wound. As she bent over him, fearing that he was dead, there came a voice through the twilight, very small and still, like music sounding from a distance, in which the notes are clear but the words are lost. The girl turned to see if someone had spoken from the window above them, but she saw no one.

Then the old man's lips began to move, as if in answer, and she heard him say in the Parthian tongue: "Not so, my Lord: For when saw I thee an hungered and fed thee? Or thirsty, and gave thee drink? When saw I thee a stranger, and took thee in? Or naked, and clothed thee? When saw I thee sick or in prison, and came unto thee? Three-and-thirty years have I looked for thee; but I have never seen thy face, nor ministered to thee, my King."

He ceased, and the sweet voice came again. And again the maid heard it, very faintly and far away. But now it seemed as though she understood the words:

"Verily I say unto thee, Inasmuch as thou hast done it unto one of the least of these my brethren, thou hast done it unto me."

A calm radiance of wonder and joy lighted the pale face of Artaban like the first ray of dawn on a snowy mountain-peak. One long, last breath of relief exhaled gently from his lips.

His journey was ended. His treasures were accepted. The Other Wise Man had found the King.

All the ends of the world shall remember and turn unto the LORD . . . For the kingdom is the LORD'S. . . . Lift up your heads, O ye gates; and be ye lift up, ye everlasting doors; and the King of glory shall come in. Who is this King of glory? The LORD strong and mighty . . . Lift up your heads, O ye gates; even lift them up, ye everlasting doors; and the King of glory shall come in. Who is this King of glory? The LORD of hosts, he is the King of glory.

--- PSALM 22:27-28, 24:7-10

OH, HOW JOYFULLY

J. FALK

Oh, how joyfully, oh, how merrily,
Christmas comes with its grace divine!
Grace again is beaming,
Christ the world redeeming:
Hail, ye Christians,
Hail the joyous Christmas time!

THE NATIVITY by Franz Christoph Janneck. Christie's Images.

God Rest Ye Merry, Gentlemen

OLD ENGLISH CAROL   OLD ENGLISH CAROL

God rest ye mer-ry, gen-tle-men, Let noth-ing you dis-may,

Re-mem-ber Christ our Sav-iour Was born on Christ-mas day,

To save us all from Sa-tan's pow'r, When we were gone a-stray.

O tid-ings of com-fort and joy, com-fort and

joy, O tid-ings of com-fort and joy.

In Bethlehem, in Israel,
This blessed Babe was born
And laid within a manger
Upon this blessed morn,
The which his mother Mary
Did nothing take in scorn.
O tidings of comfort and joy, comfort and joy!
O tidings of comfort and joy.

From God our heavenly Father
A blessed angel came
And unto certain shepherds
Brought tidings of the same,
How that in Bethlehem was born
The Son of God by name.
O tidings of comfort and joy, comfort and joy!
O tidings of comfort and joy.

The shepherds at those tidings
Rejoiced much in mind
And left their flocks afeeding
In tempest, storm, and wind,
And went to Bethlehem straitway,
The Son of God to find.
O tidings of comfort and joy, comfort and joy!
O tidings of comfort and joy.

But when to Bethlehem they came,
Whereat this infant lay,
They found him in a manger
Where oxen feed on hay,
His mother Mary kneeling
Unto the Lord did pray.
O tidings of comfort and joy, comfort and joy!
O tidings of comfort and joy.

The Second Coming

Because the beginning shall remind us of the end,

And the first Coming of the second Coming.

T.S. ELIOT

CHAPTER SEVEN

And a voice came out of the throne, saying, Praise our God, all ye his servants, and ye that fear him, both small and great. And I heard as it were the voice of a great multitude, and as the voice of many waters, and as the voice of mighty thunderings, saying, Alleluia: for the Lord God omnipotent reigneth. --- REVELATION 19:5-6

O COME, ALL YE FAITHFUL

AUTHOR UNKNOWN

O come, all ye faithful,
Joyful and triumphant,
O come ye, O come ye to Bethlehem;
Come and behold Him,
Born the King of Angels;
O come, let us adore Him,
O come, let us adore Him,
O come, let us adore Him,
Christ the Lord.

Sing, choirs of angels,
Sing in exultation;
Sing, all ye citizens of Heav'n above:
"Glory to God
All glory in the highest";

O come, let us adore Him,
O come, let us adore Him,
O come, let us adore Him,
Christ the Lord.

Yea, Lord, we greet Thee,
Born this happy morning;
Jesus, to Thee be glory giv'n,
Word of the Father,
Now in flesh appearing;
O come, let us adore Him,
O come, let us adore Him,
O come, let us adore Him,
Christ the Lord.

ADORACIÓN DE LOS PASTORES by Anton Raphael Mengs. Fine Art Photographic Library.

ANGELS AND HOLY CHILD by Marianne Stokes. Fine Art Photographic Library.

Iknow that my Redeemer liveth, and that He shall stand at the latter day upon the earth. . . . But now is Christ risen from the dead, and become the firstfruits of them that slept. For since by man came death, by man came also the resurrection of the dead. For as in Adam all die, even so in Christ shall all be made alive. --- JOB 19:25, I CORINTHIANS 15:20-22

AND THE WORD WAS MADE FLESH

LAURENCE HOUSMAN

Light looked down and beheld Darkness.
"Thither will I go," said Light.
Peace looked down and beheld War.
"Thither will I go," said Peace.
Love looked down and beheld Hatred.
"Thither will I go," said Love.
So came Light and shone.
So came Peace and gave rest.
So came Love and brought Life.

ADORATION OF THE KINGS by Filippino Lippi. Superstock.

Behold, I show you a mystery; We shall not all sleep, but we shall all be changed, In a moment, in the twinkling of an eye, at the last trump: for the trumpet shall sound, and the dead shall be raised incorruptible, and we shall be changed. . . . Then shall be brought to pass the saying that is written, Death is swallowed up in victory. O death, where is thy sting? O grave, where is thy victory?

--- I Corinthians 15:51-52, 54-55

WHO ARE THE WISE MEN?

B.Y. Williams

Who were the Wise Men in the long ago?
Not Herod, fearful lest he lose his throne;
Not Pharisees too proud to claim their own;
Not priests and scribes whose province was to know;
Not money-changers running to and fro;
But three who traveled, weary and alone,
With dauntless faith, because before them shone
The Star that led them to a manger low.

Who are the Wise Men now, when all is told?
Not men of science; not the great and strong;
Not those who wear a kingly diadem;
Not those whose eager hands pile high the gold;
But those amid the tumult and the throng
Who follow still the Star of Bethlehem.

And I beheld, and I heard the voice of many angels round about the throne . . . Saying with a loud voice, Worthy is the Lamb that was slain . . . And every creature which is in heaven, and on the earth, and under the earth . . . heard I saying, Blessing, and honour, and glory, and power, be unto him that sitteth upon the throne, and unto the Lamb for ever and ever. --- REVELATION 5:11-13

THERE'S A SONG IN THE AIR!

JOSIAH GILBERT HOLLAND

There's a song in the air!
There's a star in the sky!
There's a mother's deep prayer
And a baby's low cry!
And the star rains its fire
While the beautiful sing,
For the manger of Bethlehem
Cradles a King!

There's a tumult of joy
O'er the wonderful birth,
For the Virgin's sweet boy
Is the Lord of the earth.
Ay! the star rains its fire
While the beautiful sing,
For the manger of Bethlehem
Cradles a King!

In the light of that star
Lie the ages impearled;
And that song from afar
Has swept over the world.
Every hearth is aflame,
And the beautiful sing
In the homes of the nations
That Jesus is King!

We rejoice in the light,
And we echo the song
That comes down thro' the night
From the heavenly throng.
Ay! we shout to the lovely
Evangel they bring,
And we greet in His cradle
Our Saviour and King!

ANGELS IN A HEAVENLY LANDSCAPE by Benozzo Gozzoli. Bridgeman Art Library/Superstock.

AUTHORS

TITLES

ARTISTS

PAINTINGS

ADDITIONAL ART CREDITS

Page 7: THE NATIVITY by Santi di Tito. Canali PhotoBank Milan/Superstock. Page 30: ADORATION OF THE SHEPHERDS by Louis De Nain. Superstock. Page 47: THE ANNUNCIATION by Eustache Le Sueur. Musee du Louvre, Paris/Lauros-Giraudon, Paris/Superstock. Page 69: THE ADORATION OF THE SHEPHERDS. French School, 17th century. Christie's Images. Page 97: ADORATION OF THE KINGS by Peter Paul Rubens. Musee du Louvre, Paris/Superstock. Page 127: THE ADORATION OF THE SHEPHERDS by Jusepe de Ribera. Musee du Louvre, Paris/Giraudon, Paris/Superstock. Page 149: ANGELS IN A HEAVENLY LANDSCAPE (right hand wall) by Benozzo Gozzoli. Palazzo Medici-Riccardi, Florence, Italy/Bridgeman Art Library/Superstock.